Preser
How to Make and Use Them

by the same author

EATING IN THE OPEN

THE HOME BOOK OF ITALIAN COOKERY

Preserves
How to Make and Use Them

BERYL GOULD-MARKS

FABER & FABER
3 Queen Square
London

*First published in 1972
by Faber and Faber Limited
3 Queen Square London W C 1
Printed in Great Britain by
Western Printing Services Ltd, Bristol
All rights reserved*

ISBN 0 571 09837 1

© *Beryl Gould-Marks 1972*

For Luisa Rakowitsch

Contents

Introduction	page 9
How to Use This Book	11
Weights and Measures	12
Oven Temperatures	13
Sugar Temperatures	15

PRESERVING WITH SUGAR — 17

Jams, Fruit Butters, Cheeses and Curds — 33
Making and Using Jams, Fruit Butters, Cheeses and Curds

Jellies — 71
Making and Using Jellies

Marmalades — 95
Making and Using Marmalades

Candying — 111
Making and Using Candied Fruit, Stalks and Chestnuts

PRESERVING BY STERILISATION AND VACUUM — 123

Fruit Bottling — 129
Bottling and Using Bottled Fruit

Fruit Syrups and Juices — 137
Making and Using Fruit Syrups and Juices

CONTENTS

PRESERVING WITH VINEGAR AND SPICES

Flavoured Vinegars, Chutneys and Pickles   *page* 149
   Making and Using Vinegars, Chutneys and Pickles

PRESERVING BY DRYING

Drying Herbs and Using Dried Herbs   191
   Making and Using Tisanes (Infusions)

PRESERVING WITH ALCOHOL

Making and Using Liqueurs and Wine Infusions   201

MISCELLANEOUS

Mincemeat and Other Recipes   214

APPENDIX

Useful Pastry Recipes   219

Glossary   223

Index   227

Introduction

Like the squirrels, ancient man needed to store his food from times of plenty for the hard winters. One of his first steps towards effective community living and civilisation was the ability to preserve victuals for the ever probable seven lean years. Drying, smoking, salting, spicing, hermetically sealing and conserving by heat, cold, sugar, vinegar and alcohol, gradually evolved from haphazard empiricism to scientific knowledge. As time went by methods became more and more reliable.

Nowadays there is a growing awareness of the importance of eating foods that are naturally grown and cooked without harmful artificial colouring and injurious chemicals. It is almost too easy to buy a jar of this or that from the supermarket, but no bought jam, chutney or pickle can have the flavour of those you make yourself.

What memories are captured too. My hedgerow jelly reminds me of a lovely autumn day, with blue skies and the sun warm on my back as I picked the wild fruit. The aroma of quinces takes me to a friend's old-fashioned garden. The glistening bright orange of Seville marmalade, the first preserve of the year, brings back the crisp winter's day when I made it.

Once you have made your preserves please don't leave them on the shelves 'sitting pretty'. I know somebody who cannot bear to open her neatly capped and labelled jams. There is much more to jams and jellies than just spreading them on bread and butter. The French serve them on small plates and eat them with

INTRODUCTION

a teaspoon for dessert. The Russians add jam to their tea. Chutneys, instead of only being eaten with cold meat, can spark up many a dish.

When I make my preserves I plan how I will use them. This means that nothing hangs fire and gets pushed to the back of the store cupboard to become mouldy and senile.

This is a cookbook for those who really enjoy cooking and like to have jars and bottles filled with different coloured brews. Each section deals with a specific branch of preserving fruit, herbs or vegetables, and also gives ideas and recipes for using them, for example:

Cheese and Chutney Quiche A tart in which egg, cheese and chutney blend to make a savoury supper dish.
Wild Duck with Bigarade Sauce The sauce is made with Seville orange marmalade.
Siamese Stuffed Chicken Marries perfectly with sweet and sour chutney.
Beef Smoore with Peach Chutney A wonderful combination.
Quince Jelly Cooked with pork is a new experience. It is also a flavourful glaze for a French Apple Tart.
Bar-le-Duc Makes a mouth-watering sweet with cream cheese.
Raspberry Vinegar Poured over an old-fashioned batter pudding is an almost-forgotten joy.

These are just a few of the exciting ways you can use your preserves to open up new gastronomic horizons.

How to Use this Book

Before making preserves read the introduction to each section. This gives a simple explanation of basic methods, and ways of solving problems.

'Pointers to Success' give a summary of the important factors and things to look out for.

The first page of each section gives a list of the contents in their order to help you to find what you want quickly.

The Glossary at the end of the book gives simple explanations of technical and scientific terms connected with the various processes of preserving. It also defines some culinary words.

The recipes for using preserves suggest ways in which you can incorporate them into your repertoire. It is hoped that they will stimulate you to find even more ways of using them.

All spoon measures are level, unless otherwise stated.

Note: When some vegetables are bottled the acid content can be so low that there is a danger of botulism (see Glossary, page 223). For this reason no recipes for bottling vegetables are included.

Weights and Measures

APPROXIMATE METRIC EQUIVALENTS OF AVOIRDUPOIS WEIGHTS

N.B. These figures are proportional and are worked out to the nearest round figure.

Weight

1 oz.	= 28·5 grammes
4 oz.	= 114 grammes
8 oz	= 225·5 grammes
1 lb.	= 451 grammes
1 lb. 1½ oz.	= 500 grammes (½ kilogramme)
2 lb. 3 oz.	= 1,000 grammes (1 kilogramme)

APPROXIMATE METRIC EQUIVALENTS OF BRITISH MEASURES OF CAPACITY

1 gill or 5 fluid oz.	= ·142 litre
4 gills or 20 fluid oz. or 1 pint	= ·568 litre
1¾ pints	= 1 litre
2 pints or 1 quart	= 1·136 litres

LINEAR MEASURES

1 inch	= 2·54 centimetres

WEIGHTS AND MEASURES

4 inches	= 10 centimetres (approximately)
12 inches or 1 foot	= 0·3048 metre
36 inches, 3 feet or 1 yard	= 0·914 metre
40 inches (approximately)	= 1 metre

CENTIGRADE AND FAHRENHEIT EQUIVALENTS

To convert Centigrade into Fahrenheit: multiply by 9, divide by 5, and add 32.

To convert Fahrenheit into Centigrade: subtract 32, multiply by 5, and divide by 9.

Centigrade	*Fahrenheit*
0°	32°
20°	68°
40°	104°
60°	140°
80°	176°
100°	212°

OVEN TEMPERATURES
(approximate equivalents)

Degrees centigrade	*Gas setting*	*Electric Setting* (Fahrenheit)
120	¼	250
130	½	250
145	1	300
155	2	300
170	3	350
180	4	350
195	5	375

WEIGHTS AND MEASURES

205	6	400
220	7	425
230	8	450
245	9	475

Water boils at 212°F or 100°C
Blood heat is approximately 98°F or 37°C

SUGAR TEMPERATURES

104·4°C or 220°F		For jam, jelly and marmalade	See page 26 for setting point tests.
107·2°C or 225°F	Thread	For sugar syrups	Runny and sticky.
110°C or 230°F	Pearl	For some icings	A little poured into cold water forms small, pearl-like balls.
112·7°C or 235°F	Feather	For some icings	A little poured into cold water forms bubbles which float.
114·4°C or 238°F	Soft Ball	For fudges, American type frostings, some fondants	A little poured into cold water forms soft ball when rolled between fingers.
118·3°C or 245°F 121·1°C or 250°F	Hard Ball	For caramels, soft toffee, nougat	A little poured into cold water forms hard ball when rolled between fingers.
137·7°C or 280°F	Crack	For toffee	A little poured into cold water forms hard threads which bend without breaking.
143·3°C or 290°F	Hard Crack	For butterscotch, barley sugar, boiled sweets, some toffee, some caramels	A little poured into cold water forms threads which are hard and brittle.
155·5°C or 312°F	Caramel	For lining moulds and dishes. For colouring sauces and soups	Sugar becomes deep brown and brittle in cold water.

Preserving With Sugar

Introduction and General Information

Jams, Fruit Butters, Cheeses and Curds
*Making and Using Jams, Fruit Butters,
Cheeses and Curds*

Jellies
Making and Using Jellies

Marmalades
Making and Using Marmalades

Candying
*Making and Using Candied Fruit,
Stalks and Chestnuts*

INTRODUCTION AND GENERAL INFORMATION

Jams, jellies and marmalades are made and preserved by the use of sugar and heat. The best results are got from using first-rate fruit that is just ripe. It should be cooked as soon as possible after picking because pectin – the sticky substance which helps the preserve to set – deteriorates quickly. It is easier to make small quantities at a time as the operation is more maneagable. When jelly is being made, once the sugar is added rapid boiling is necessary to get a sugar concentration of 60–65 per cent, i.e. to get a firm gel. When a large quantity is made, the sugar may caramelise before setting point is reached. Caramelisation spoils flavour and colour.

(If you have a garden with fruit trees, windfalls need not be wasted, they can be used for making fruit juices, syrups and chutneys. Any bruised parts should be cut away.)

There is no need to have much special equipment, apart from scales, your largest strong saucepan, a wooden spoon and a good pouring jug. If you intend to do a lot of preserving, the following list will help to make it easier.

EQUIPMENT

Basin A fairly large basin to take the juice that drips from the jelly bag. One with graduations marked on the side, to show the amount of liquid, saves measuring the juice in a jug.

Cherry Pitter   Makes stone-removal easy.

Jam Dip Stick   See volume test (page 27).

Jam Funnel   There are special ones on the market. They are not essential but a great help when filling the pots.

Jam Pot Covers   Packets of 1-lb. and 2-lb. sizes can be bought. They contain waxed discs, cellophane covers, rubber bands and labels (see page 29).

Jars   You will probably not have to buy these, because any wide-topped jar will do. The 1-lb. squat honey jars are excellent and a good shape. Do save small jars for jelly. Once a jar of jelly is opened it may 'weep' or go 'runny' if left open for any length of time (see page 74).

Jelly Bag   These can be bought, or made at home. Special stands can be bought too, but the bag can be slung between the legs of an upturned chair or stool and the bowl placed on the upturned seat. I hang mine on the rack over the cooker when it is not in use overnight. If you make your own bag, get a large square piece of flannel, or cotton material, such as an old sheet, or three or four layers of butter muslin. Sew it strongly as liquid is heavy. You can bind the top of the bag with tape and sew loops on each corner for easy hanging. The bag should be scalded immediately before and after using, to destroy bacteria. Be sure it has no smell of soap or detergents. It must be large enough to hold the contents of your saucepan – err on the generous side when making.

Jug   This should be heatproof, but not metal as the handle gets too hot. It should have a wide pouring mouth.

Knives   Choose sharp, stainless steel for preparing fruit. A potato peeler is useful for peeling apples, pears, etc.

Paraffin Wax   Useful for sealing jars (see page 29).

Preserving Pan or Saucepan   I like a heavy stainless steel one. Good quality heavy aluminium or enamel saucepans are suitable. If you use aluminium never leave jam or chutneys in it overnight because acids attack the metal. Chipped enamel saucepans should not be used. Choose a really large pan; it must be able to hold at least double the quantity of the largest amount you are likely to make. When the sugar is added it boils up; and if the pan is too small, it boils over.

Scales Ordinary household scales.

Stone-basket A useful little wire basket which clips on to the side of the pan and hangs over the jam. As the fruit stones rise to the surface, remove them with a spoon and put them in the basket. The juice drips through, so there is no loss or mess.

Spoons To avoid burnt fingers have long-handled wooden spoons for stirring. A perforated metal spoon with a long handle is useful for removing pips, stones and scum.

Sugar Thermometer (See page 27).

FRUIT

As already mentioned, fruit for jams and jellies should be of first rate quality and just ripe. It should be used as soon as possible after it has been picked or bought. It will be higher in pectin content (see page 23) and the flavour and colour better. Fruit should be cooked initially without sugar to release the pectin and acid. The skins must be tender – no amount of cooking once sugar is added will soften them. If you want to make jam or jelly with fruit that is low in pectin, you can add another fruit which is high in pectin (see page 25) instead of adding a pectin booster (see page 24).

SUGAR

The amount of sugar used is very important. It is the sugar which preserves the fruit. If you do not use enough the preserve will not set, and if you use too much it will be too sweet and may crystallise. Both refined cane or beet sugars are suitable and you can use lump, granulated or preserving sugar. Granulated is slightly cheaper, but it does sometimes produce more scum. For shows and competitions, do use preserving sugar. It has large white crystals and gives a clear, bright preserve. It needs less stirring to prevent burning when it is dissolving, because it does not settle in a dense mass at the bottom of the pan, and it produces very little scum. Scum is not at all harmful but it may cause a cloudy preserve. It should be removed with a perforated metal spoon when setting point is reached and not before.

The sugar can be warmed in the oven before being added to the preserve, to help it to dissolve quickly. I find it quite sufficient to add the sugar to the hot jam or jelly, stir until it dissolves, then bring it quickly to boiling point and let it boil vigorously until setting point is reached. Once the jam or jelly has reached a fast boil it is generally better not to stir it.

Wholefood fans will like to use brown sugar. The flavour is much stronger and intrudes, and the colour of the preserve will be affected. It can be used with advantage for a dark chunky marmalade (see page 99).

Thin honey can be used, i.e. 8 oz. honey or 8 oz. sugar.

Glucose This may be added to sugar syrups to prevent crystallisation (see Glossary, page 223). It is uneconomical for jam making as it is expensive and less sweet than sugar.

However, if you want to use it do not cut down the sugar in the recipe by more than half.

WATER

The amount of water needed will vary according to the type of fruit, and how long it needs to be cooked to soften it before sugar is added. The size and shape of your preserving pan makes a difference too. A shallow pan will need more water as evaporation is quicker.

When you want to make twice the quantity of preserve given in a recipe *do not* double the amount of water, but use slightly less. Some fruits, like strawberries and raspberries, can be preserved without any water. Harder fruit, like apples, apricots, and plums, need water but do not swamp them.

The softest water should be used, so if you have a water softener do use it for all preserves. Hard water slows down the release of pectin from the fruit's cell walls. It can also affect the flavour and colour.

PECTIN

Pectin is a gum-like substance contained in the cell walls of fruit. A combination of pectin, sugar and acid is necessary to enable jam, jelly and marmalade to gel. It is the first slow cooking of the fruit before the sugar is added that helps to draw out the pectin. The quantity of pectin varies considerably from fruit to fruit, and according to degree of ripeness and even the weather. As the fruit matures the pectin is gradually transformed into pectic acid; this reduces the setting property of the fruit. Pectin develops from a low level in unripe fruit to its maximum when the fruit is just ripe. You will notice when cooking some fruits that the juice is quite viscous; this denotes pectin, which is a carbohydrate.

Table of Relative Pectin Content of Fruit

This table is variable, depending on the actual species of the fruit, its ripeness, and the year, i.e. dry and hot, or wet and cold weather.

High Pectin Black, red and white currants, sharp apples, Morello cherries, damsons, gooseberries, quinces, lemons. Pips from citrus fruits and the white pith (albedo) contain a good amount of pectin and should be used when marmalade is made (see page 96).
Medium Pectin Apricots, early wild and cultivated blackberries, greengages, loganberries, peaches, some varieties of plums.
Low Pectin Cherries (except Morello), pears, strawberries (most varieties).

High Pectin Fruit	allow	$1\frac{1}{4}$–$1\frac{1}{2}$ lb. sugar per 1 lb. fruit
Medium Pectin Fruit	allow	1 lb. sugar per 1 lb. fruit
Low Pectin Fruit	allow	$\frac{3}{4}$ lb. sugar per 1 lb. fruit
Citrus Fruit	allow	$1\frac{1}{2}$–2 lb. sugar per 1 lb. fruit

Pectin Boosters

When you make jam or jelly from fruit low in pectin and acid, it will need a booster to make it gel. This can be:

INTRODUCTION

lemon juice – allow 2 tablespoons to 4 lb. fruit
1 gill pectin stock to 4 lb. fruit
citric or tartaric acid ½ teaspoon to 4 lb. fruit

commercial pectin, available in liquid or powder form; liquid, 2–4 oz. to each 1 lb. fruit; powdered, ½ oz. to each 1 lb. fruit

Do read instructions on bottle or packet as these vary. Powdered is preferable because it has a longer shelf life. The liquid once opened should be used within a short period. Too much commercial pectin can ruin the flavour and colour of preserves. I prefer to use lemon juice or pectin stock.

To make pectin stock

Fruits low in pectin are also often low in acid. You can combine two fruits blending high and low pectin such as blackberry and apple, marrow and damson, strawberry and gooseberry to get a good setting jam or you can add pectin stock. Pectin stock can be made from redcurrants, gooseberries, or tart cooking apples which are rich in acid and pectin.

1 lb. redcurrants or just-ripe green gooseberries or tart apples
½ pint water

Wash the fruit. Cut up apples if making apple pectin stock. Put the fruit in a saucepan. Add the water, bring it to the boil and simmer until the fruit is soft. Press the fruit with a wooden spoon while it is cooking to help the juice to run. Strain it through a jelly bag. Put the strained juice back into the pan, bring it to the boil. Pour it into hot jars. These should either fasten with rubber rings and a screwband, or with clips or grips. Dip the rubber rings in boiling water, fix them on the jars, then fasten down the jars with screw tops, or clips or grips. When you use screwbands, tighten them, then unscrew ¼ turn. This allows for expansion. Put the jars in a pan with a false bottom, or on a rack in the pan. Fill up with water; the jars should be covered with water. Bring slowly to boiling point, boil for 5 minutes. Remove jars, screw up tightly if using screwband tops. Cool for 24 hours, tighten screw tops if necessary. Test to see if properly sealed. Remove screwbands or clips, lift each jar by the lid. If the seal is complete the lid will remain intact.

If you intend to use the pectin stock at once and not to keep it, there is no need to sterilise the jars.

Testing Fruit for Pectin Content

If it amuses you to make scientific experiments, you may like to try this simple test. It will help you to find out how much pectin there is in the fruit you are going to use.

Cook a little of the fruit until it softens, then put 1 teaspoon of the juice in a small jar. Let it cool, then add 3 teaspoons of methylated spirits. Shake to mix. Leave for 1 minute. If fruit is rich in pectin the jelly formed will be firm and transparent. If pectin is moderate it will be less firm and easily broken into two or three pieces. When supply of pectin is poor the jelly breaks up into tiny pieces.

TESTS FOR SETTING POINT

Tests for setting point should begin when the liquid begins to thicken. The time varies according to the type of fruit being cooked – anything from 5 to 15 minutes. There are several ways of testing it.

Flake Test Dip a wooden spoon into the preserve, take it out, turn it round over the pan; the preserve should cling to the spoon as it cools and it should have already begun to set. Tip the spoon sideways so that the mixture can run off. The drops should run together and form flakes which fall off cleanly.

Saucer Test Spoon a little of the preserve on to a saucer, let it cool. When setting point has been reached, the preserve wrinkles when pushed gently with the finger.

Sugar Thermometer This is the most accurate way of testing for setting point. Put the thermometer in very hot or boiling water and then dry it before putting it in the preserve. Stir the jam gently. Put in the thermometer, but do not let the glass bulb rest on the bottom of the pan – it could break. Read the temperature at eye level. It should register 220·7°F (8·7°F above boiling point of water); the sugar should have reached a concentration of 65 per cent when setting point is reached. If by any chance the bulb breaks and the mercury get into the preserve, scrap the lot. When you take the thermometer out of the hot liquid, put it at once into boiling water. Dry it carefully and keep it in a safe place.

VOLUME TEST WITH JAM DIP STICK

To make a dip stick Take a wooden spoon with a long handle, or a wooden stick. Allow a 1-lb. jam jar full of water for each 1 lb. of jam you are going to make. For example if you are going to make 5 lb. of jam, measure 5 1-lb. jars of water into your preserving pan. Hold the spoon or stick upright in the water and make a notch at the water level. Get rid of the water. When making jam and you think setting point has been reached, take the pan off the heat. Use your jam dip stick like a car dip stick. Put it in the jam; if it has reduced to the notch of the stick, setting point should have been reached; if not, let it boil a little longer.

YIELD

5 lb. preserve is usually made from 3 lb. added sugar. To find out easily how much yield any quantity of added sugar should give, multiply the weight of the sugar by 5 and divide the result by 3. The answer is the correct yield of preserve. For example, 5 lb. sugar $\times$ 5 = 25. Divide by 3 = $8\frac{1}{3}$ lb. preserve.

POTTING

Use a work study method to decide the best position for the jars in relation to the saucepan, so that filling up requires the minimum effort combined with maximum convenience and safety

While the preserve is cooking and the scrupulously clean jars are warming in the oven (if they are cold, the hot jam might crack them), put several sheets of newspaper on the table. When the preserve has reached setting point, arrange the jars on the paper, then carefully carry the pan from stove to table. Dip in the jug or spouted ladle and fill up the jars to the brim – unless you are sealing with paraffin wax (see below), when about $\frac{1}{4}$ in. should be left for the wax. Immediately put on discs (see below), which should be exactly the right size. Press them down lightly (waxed side downwards), so that all air is excluded. The covers should be put on while the preserve is hot or when it is quite cold, otherwise there may be condensation, which causes mould. Wipe the rims and sides of the jars with a damp cloth.

It is tempting to use the screw tops which come on some commercial jars, but if there is any moisture between the metal and the cardboard lining it can cause mould. Patent airtight cellophane covers can be bought; or use the transparent covers in the packets of jam pot covers (see page 20) containing these, and waxed discs, that can usually be bought from a stationer. Moisten the cellophane covers on the side away from the preserve.

PARAFFIN WAX

This makes a good airtight cover. It can be bought from the chemist's. Heat it over a low heat; on no account should it be overheated. Put it in a small jug or an old teapot, one that pours well. Fill the jars (see above). Put the usual waxed discs (see Potting above) on the preserve before pouring on the paraffin wax. Medicinal liquid paraffin can be mixed with the wax to make it less brittle – 1 part liquid paraffin to 3 parts melted wax. Carefully pour or spoon on the wax. As the preserve cools, the wax is drawn down in the centre and causes a hollow. This should be covered with another layer of melted wax. Let some of the wax go over the sides of the jars to ensure a complete seal. When the wax is quite cold and hard, cover it with greaseproof paper and tie down. When you open the jar of preserve do not throw away the paraffin wax, but wash it and keep it for another batch.

LABELLING

Do remember to label all jars clearly with the name of the preserve and the date. It is very frustrating to open a jar and find it is chutney and not jam. It is not always possible to see from the outside.

STORAGE

Store if possible in a cool, dark, well-ventilated cupboard. Heat can cause shrinkage, and damp can be another reason for mould.

POINTERS TO SUCCESS

- Use best quality, just-ripe fruit.

- Cook fruit gently until skins are tender before adding sugar.

- Add the required amount of sugar when fruit is softened. Do not use less sugar (exception, low-sugar jam, page 50). Too little sugar can be the cause of fermentation. Let sugar dissolve, then boil rapidly until setting point is reached.

- Whole fruit jam should cool in the pan a little, then stir and pot. As the liquid begins to set, it surrounds the fruit and keeps it suspended instead of rising in the jar.

INTRODUCTION

- Overboiling spoils colour and flavour, but fermentation can be caused if jam is not sufficiently boiled.

- Always put a waxed disc on the jam as soon as the jar is filled.

- Make certain there is enough pectin to get a good firm gel. You can always replace lemon juice with pectin stock or commercial pectin (see pages 25–6).

Jams, Fruit Butters, Cheeses and Curds

JAMS

Normandy Apple Conserve
Apricot Jam made with Fresh Apricots
Dried Apricot Jam
Bar-le-Duc
Blackberry and Apple Jam
Blackcurrant Jam
Carrot and Almond Preserve
Black Cherry Jam
Imperial Cherry Jam
Morello Cherry Jam
Chestnut Jam
Cotignac (Quince and Orange Preserve)
Cranberry Conserve
Gooseberry Bar-le-Duc
Gooseberry and Elderflower Jam
Gooseberry Jam
Greengage Jam
Marrow and Ginger Jam
Mulberry Jam
Orange and White Cherry Conserve
Passion Fruit and Peach Jam
Plum and Apple Jam
Pumpkin Preserve
Quince Jelly Jam
Raspberry Jam
Seedless Raspberry Jam
Red Rose Petal Conserve
Rhubarb and Dried Fig Jam
Rhubarb and Orange Jam
Common Strawberry Jam
Whole Strawberry Jam
Low Sugar Jams

FRUIT BUTTERS, CHEESES AND CURDS

Fruit Butters
Fruit Cheeses
Fruit Curds
Apple Butter

Damson Cheese
Lemon Curd
Orange Curd
Quince Cheese

SAVOURY RECIPES USING JAM

Braised Lamb Chops
Gooseberry Sauce

Minced Ham with Cherry Sauce
Partidges with Cherry Sauce

SWEET RECIPES USING JAM

Banana Trifle
Bread and Butter Fritters
Cream Cheese Bar-le-Duc
Croûtes aux Cerises
Curd or Jam Puffs
Guards' Pudding
Jam Beignets
Jam Turnovers
Lemon Curd and Apple Pie
Mirlitons (Macaroon Tarts)
Normandy Pudding

Poor Man's Baked Omelette
Raspberry Buns
Raspberry Custard Ice
Raspberry Noyau
Rose Petal Cake
Rouleau Rouennais (Rouen Rolypoly)
Witches' Froth

Blackcurrant Tea

JAMS

Normandy Apple Conserve

4 *lb. cooking apples (preferably ones that do not break up easily)*
3 *lb. sugar*
1 *pint water*
2 *oz. currants*
2 *oz. sultanas*
2 *oz. chopped candied orange peel*
juice of 2 *lemons*
2 *tablespoons rum*

Boil sugar and water together for 20 minutes. Peel, core and slice the apples. Add apples, currants, sultanas, candied peel and lemon juice to the syrup. Cook gently, stirring from time to time to prevent burning. Cook until the apple slices are brown and shiny but have not broken up. Stir in the rum. Pot and cover.

Apricot Jam made with Fresh Apricots

2 *lb. apricots*
2 *lb. sugar*
$\frac{3}{4}$ *pint water*
juice of 1 *large lemon*

Choose just-ripe apricots. Wipe them and cut in half. Remove the stones, save half of them and use their kernels in the jam. Cook the apricots gently in the water and lemon juice until they have softened. Crack the stones with nutcrackers; if the brown skin does not come off easily, pop the kernels in hot water for a minute. Add them to the jam. When the apricots are quite tender, add the sugar, stir until it is dissolved. Boil until setting point is reached. Remove scum if necessary. Let the jam cool a little, stir to distribute fruit. Pot and cover.

Dried Apricot Jam

1 *lb. best dried apricots*
3 *lb. sugar*
3 *pints water*

1 *oz. chopped blanched almonds*
iuice of 1 *large lemon*

Cut up the fruit, soak it in the 3 pints of water for 24 hours. The next day, put the apricots with the water they were soaked in into a pan. Cook gently for about 30 minutes or until they are tender. Add sugar, lemon juice and almonds. Stir until sugar is dissolved. Boil until setting point is reached. Stir occasionally as this jam is apt to catch. Remove scum if necessary. Pot and cover.

Bar-le-Duc

This famous French jam which originally came from Bar-le-Duc in Lorraine is very delicate and delicious. It can be made from white or red currants or a mixture of both. To make it properly you need a lot of patience because each currant should be pricked so that the sugar syrup penetrates the currants, which prevents them from becoming shrivelled and keeps them plump. Some people in France, I am told, remove all the pips with a quill toothpick or the sharpened plume from a goose. The quill is put in at the stem end and the pips extracted. We can make a very good jam without being quite so perfectionist.

2 *lb. white or red currants*   3 *lb. sugar*

Remove the stalks from the currants, wash them and drain. Prick each one gently. Put them in a preserving pan with the sugar. Leave overnight. The next day bring it very slowly to the boil, and boil for 3 minutes. Leave until a skin begins to form, stir gently to distribute the fruit, then pot and cover.

Blackberry and Apple Jam

If possible use wild blackberries as they have a much better flavour, and the apples should be sharp. I prefer to cook the two fruits separately at first as they need different times to soften.

2 lb. blackberries *½ pint water*
1½ lb. apples *3 lb. sugar*

Wash and pick over the blackberries, cook them in ¼ pint of water until soft. Peel, core and slice the apples, cook them in the rest of the water until they soften. Mix the two fruits together, add the sugar, stir until dissolved, then boil rapidly until setting point is reached. Pot and cover.

Blackcurrant Jam

As blackcurrants are so rich in pectin they need no booster. The vitamin C is not destroyed by cooking. As they are sharp they will need more sugar than most jams.

2 lb. blackcurrants *3 lb. sugar*
1½ pints water

Strip the currants from the stalks with a fork. Wash them if they are dusty. Put them with the water in a pan, bring slowly to the boil, then simmer until their skins are really tender – this may take 30 minutes or longer. It is important because if the sugar is added before the skins are soft, they will remain hard. Stir from time to time. Add the sugar, stir until it is dissolved, bring to the boil and continue to boil until setting point is reached. Skim if necessary, leave the jam in the pan until a skin begins to form on top. Pot and cover.

Carrot and Almond Preserve

3 lb. cleaned, chopped young carrots
water
grated rind and juice of limes or lemons
1 lb. sugar to each 1 lb carrot purée
1 oz. roughly chopped blanched almonds
1 tablespoon rum to each 1 lb. purée

Just cover the carrots with water and simmer them until they are soft. Rub them through a sieve or liquidise them. Weigh the purée and to every pound allow 1 lb. sugar, the grated rind of 1 lime or lemon and 1 tablespoon of lime or lemon juice. Simmer gently until the preserve is thick and comes away from the sides of the saucepan. Stir in the rum and almonds. Pot and cover.

Black Cherry Jam

3 lb. firm, just-ripe black cherries
6 tablespoons lemon juice
2½ lb. sugar

Remove stalks from cherries, stone and wash them. Drain well. Put the cherries in a bowl, add the lemon juice, cover with sugar. Leave overnight. Strain off the syrup into the pan, stir over a low heat until sugar is completely dissolved. Bring to the boil, add the cherries and cook for 10–20 minutes. Begin to test for setting point every 5 minutes. Remove any scum, leave the jam to cool a little, stir to distribute fruit. Pot and cover.

Imperial Cherry Jam

In this French recipe the cherries are cooked in redcurrant and raspberry juice. The jam has a wonderful flavour.

½ *lb. redcurrants*
½ *lb. raspberries*
1 *gill water*

2 *lb. firm red cherries*
2½ *lb. sugar*

Pick over and wash the currants and raspberries. Cook them gently in the water until they are soft. Press with a wooden spoon to extract the juice. Strain overnight in a jelly bag. Stone the cherries, cook them in the redcurrant and raspberry juice until they are quite soft. Add the sugar, stir until it is dissolved. Bring to the boil, and boil until setting point is reached. Pot and cover.

Morello Cherry Jam

This cherry jam needs more sugar. Allow 1½ lb. to each 1 lb. of just-ripe fruit.

1 *lb. Morello cherries*
1½ *lb. sugar*

juice of 1 *small lemon*
a little water

Remove stalks from cherries, wash and stone them. Drain well.

Put them in a pan with a little water. Cook them gently until they have softened. Add the sugar and lemon juice, stir until the sugar is dissolved. Boil vigorously until setting point is reached. Pot and cover.

Chestnut Jam

2 *lb. Italian or Spanish chestnuts*
1½ *lb. granulated sugar*
½ *pint water*
1 *teaspoon vanilla essence or* 1–2 *tablespoons brandy*

Make a large nick on the flat side of the chestnuts. Put them in cold water and bring to the boil. Turn off the heat. As soon as you can handle the chestnuts without burning your fingers, remove the two skins. This is easier if done while the nuts are still warm. Cook them in boiling water until they are soft. Drain, and liquidise, or rub through a sieve, or put through a vegetable mill. Dissolve the sugar in the water, bring to the boil and cook until the syrup falls in flakes from the spoon or reaches 220°–222°F. Add the chestnut purée and simmer gently until the mixture thickens and comes away from the sides of the saucepan. Stir in the vanilla essence or brandy. Pot in small jars, cover and store. Serve as a sweet with whipped cream or as a cake or sandwich filling.

Cotignac
(Quince and Orange Preserve)

This is a delicious, very thick preserve made with quinces and oranges. It is a speciality of Orleans and legend says that it was offered to Joan of Arc as she entered the city. This was a special mark of honour. It is often eaten with unsalted cream cheese in France and makes a good sweet.

10 *lb. quinces*	*water*
5 *large oranges*	1 *lb. sugar to each* 1 *lb. purée*
juice of 2 *large lemons*	

Wipe 5 lb. of the quinces, cut them up but do not bother to peel or core them. Put them in a heavy pan, just cover with water, bring to the boil, then cook gently until they are really soft. Strain and squeeze out all the juice. Peel, core and slice the other 5 lb. of quinces. Peel, quarter and remove pips from the oranges. Tie the pips in a muslin bag. Add quinces, oranges and lemon juice to the quince juice. Bring to the boil and simmer gently until fruit is soft. Liquidise and pass through a sieve; or put through a vegetable mill. Weigh the purée and allow 1 lb. sugar per pound. Put sugar and purée into the pan, stir until sugar is dissolved. Cook slowly until mixture is very thick and comes away from the sides of the pan. If a line is made across the bottom of the pan and does not fill in, the preserve is sufficiently cooked. Spoon into warm jars, pressing down to avoid air pockets. Cover and store.

Cranberry Conserve

1 *lb. cranberries*	2 *oz. chopped seedless raisins*
½ *pint boiling water*	2 *oz. chopped walnuts*
¾ *lb. sugar*	1 *sweet orange*

Wash the cranberries, cover them with boiling water, cook until tender. Rub through a nylon sieve or liquidise. Put the purée back into the pan, add sugar, raisins and walnuts, stir until sugar is dissolved. Stir frequently. When mixture boils, add the washed and thinly sliced orange. Cook gently until mixture thickens and setting point is reached. Pot and cover. This goes well with game.

Gooseberry Bar-le-Duc

3 lb. barely ripe green gooseberries *½ pint white wine vinegar*
4 lb. sugar

Top and tail the gooseberries. Wash them, let them drain. Put them in the pan with the vinegar and heat slowly. Add half the sugar, bring to the boil. Simmer for 20 minutes. Add the rest of the sugar, stir until it is dissolved. Cook gently until the mixture has thickened and setting point is reached. Pot and cover.

Gooseberry and Elderflower Jam

2 lb. just-ripe green gooseberries *6 large heads of elderflowers*
2 lb. sugar   *(picked early in the morning on*
1 pint water   *a dry day)*

Top, tail and wash gooseberries. Gently wash the elderflowers. Tie them in muslin. Put the gooseberries, water and elderflowers in the pan, simmer gently until the fruit is quite soft. Add the sugar, stir until it is dissolved. Boil vigorously until setting point is reached. Stir frequently to prevent burning. Remove the elderflowers and any scum. Pot and cover.

Gooseberry Jam

Can be made in the same way as above, but without the addition of the elderflowers.

Greengage Jam

3 *lb. just-ripe greengages*
3 *lb. sugar*

1–2 *gills of water (depending on juiciness of fruit)*

Wipe the greengages, cut them in half, remove stones. A few of the stones can be cracked and the skinned kernels added if liked. Put the fruit in a pan, add the water and simmer until skins are soft. Add sugar, stir until it is dissolved, add kernels if to be used, and bring to the boil. Boil vigorously until setting point is reached. If preferred the stones need not be removed before cooking, but can be taken out as they come to the surface of the jam. A stone-basket is useful (see page 21). Pot and cover.

Marrow and Ginger Jam

2 *lb. marrow (weighed after peeling)*
2 *tablespoons lemon juice*

2 *oz. chopped preserved stem ginger and some of the syrup*
1½ *lb. sugar*

Remove seeds and cut the marrow into small cubes. Steam it over hot water until it is tender. Put it in a bowl, cover with the sugar, leave overnight. The next day put it in a pan with the ginger, syrup and lemon juice. Cook gently until the marrow is translucent and the jam thick. Test by the volume test (see page 27) or use a thermometer (see page 27). Pot and cover. This is delicious added to fruit salads.

Mulberry Jam

Unfortunately mulberries seem to be getting scarcer and scarcer. They make an excellent jam or jelly (see also page 80).

2 lb. mulberries (they should be just ripe)
½ pint water
1½ lb. sugar
1 tablespoon lemon juice

Pick over the fruit, remove stalks, wash and drain. Put the mulberries and water in a pan, cook gently until they have softened. Add lemon juice and sugar, stir until dissolved, then boil until jam reaches setting point. Remove scum, leave to cool slightly, stir to distribute fruit. Pot and cover.

Orange and White Cherry Conserve

3 lb. whiteheart cherries
2½ lb. sugar
3 large thin-skinned oranges
juice of 1 small lemon

Wash the cherries, remove stems and stones. Wash the oranges, slice them finely on a plate so that the juice is not lost. Remove any pips and tie them loosely in a muslin bag. Put the cherries, oranges, pips and the orange and lemon juice into a pan. Bring to the boil, add the sugar, stir until it is dissolved. Cook slowly until the jam is very thick. Remove pips. Pot and cover.

Passion Fruit and Peach Jam

10–12 *passion fruit*
6–8 *peaches*
lemon juice
1 *lb. sugar to each* 1 *pint pulp*

Cut the passion fruit in half transversely and scoop out all the inside. Peel the peaches, discard the stones, chop up the flesh. Measure the passion fruit pulp and chopped peaches in a jug and for each 1 pint allow 1 lb. sugar and the juice of 1 lemon. Put all the ingredients into a pan, stir over a low heat until the sugar is dissolved. Bring to the boil and cook until the jam sets. Pot and cover.

Plum and Apple Jam

This need not be the rather nasty jam the wartime song told about, but can be quite good. If you have both plum and apple trees it is well worth making.

$1\frac{1}{2}$ *lb. plums*
$1\frac{1}{2}$ *lb. apples (weighed after peeling and coring)*
$\frac{3}{4}$ *pint water*
3 *lb. sugar*

Wash the plums, cut in half and remove stones. Chop the apples. Put the fruit in a pan, add water and cook gently until the plum skins are quite soft. Add sugar, stir until dissolved, bring to the boil, then boil rapidly until setting point is reached. Pot and cover.

Pumpkin Preserve

Only make a small quantity of this jam. It is unusual, rather exotic, and you may not like it.

1 *lb. pumpkin (weighed without skin or seeds)*
1 *lb. sugar*
½ *teaspoon powdered cardamoms*
1 *fluid oz. rosewater (obtainable at a chemist's)*
juice of 1 *large lemon*

Grate the pumpkin coarsely, put it in a scalded white cloth and squeeze it to get rid of some of the liquid. Put it in a pan with the sugar and lemon juice, stir until sugar is dissolved, add cardamoms, stir and cook until it is thick, then stir in the rosewater. Pot and cover.

Quince Jelly Jam

This is a wonderful jam. It looks most attractive, as translucent pieces of quince are caught in the red jelly, and the taste too is exceptional. It makes excellent small tartlets.

4 *lb. just-ripe quinces plus* 3 *small, carefully-chosen, perfect quinces*
6 *pints water*
1 *lb. sugar to each* 1 *pint juice*
2 *tablespoons lemon juice*

Make the jelly first. Wipe the quinces thoroughly to remove fuzz. Cut up the 4 lb. of quinces, but do not peel or core them. Put them in the pan, add the water and cook slowly until the fruit is soft. This will take about 1 hour. Strain through a jelly bag overnight. The next day, peel and core the 3 quinces and cut them into eighths lengthwise. Cover with cold water and simmer until softened. Drain. Measure the strained juice, heat it, add the sugar (1 lb. to each pint of juice), add the lemon juice. Stir until the sugar is dissolved, add the quince pieces, bring to the boil and boil gently until setting point is reached. Remove scum if necessary. Let the jam cool a little before potting, so that the pieces of fruit are suspended in the jelly. Stir to distribute them evenly, then pot and cover.

Raspberry Jam

This is useful for small quantities of raspberries.

equal quantities of raspberries and
  sugar

Pick over the raspberries, hull and wash them, drain. Put them in a shallow fireproof dish. Put the sugar in a bowl. Put them both in a medium hot oven (350°F) and let them heat through, but watch to make sure that the sugar does not brown or the fruit dry up. When they are both quite hot, remove from oven, put both together in a heavy pan. Heat gently, stirring until the sugar is completely dissolved. Let it come to the boil, then pot and cover.

Seedless Raspberry Jam

If you object to the seeds in raspberry jam but like the flavour, try this recipe.

1 lb. raspberries   *a little water*
1 lb. sharp apples   *1 lb. sugar to each pint of purée*

Wash, but do not peel or core, the apples. Chop them up roughly. Put them in a pan, add a very little water, cook slowly until they have softened. Pick over the raspberries, hull them, wash and drain, add them to the apple and cook slowly to get a thick purée. Rub the purée through a very fine nylon sieve (a metal one can give a 'taste'). Measure the purée, put it in a pan, add the sugar, stir until dissolved over a low heat. Boil for 10–15 minutes until setting point is reached. Pot and cover.

Red Rose Petal Conserve

Choose deep red, heavily scented old-fashioned roses. Pick full grown ones early in the morning when the dew has dried on them. Perfume makers always choose the mature ones because they know that the scent is more powerful than in the young buds. Take each petal carefully from the flower. If there is any white at the base of the petals, cut it away; it can be bitter. You will need at least 6 oz. rose petals.

6 oz. scented red rose petals *½ pint water*
1½ lb. loaf sugar *2 tablespoons lemon juice*

Put the sugar and water into a heavy pan, bring to the boil, then simmer until the syrup is thick; or if you have a thermometer it should register 220°F. Add the lemon juice and rose petals. Cook them very slowly, stirring all the time until the conserve is very thick. This may take 30–45 minutes. Fill miniature jars and cover at once.

This is delicious spread on thin slices of bread and butter or it can be used in the Rose Petal Cake (see page 67).

Rhubarb and Dried Fig Jam

As rhubarb contains very little pectin, lemon juice or pectin stock must be added (see page 25).

2 *lb. rhubarb*	½ *lb. dried figs*
2 *lb. sugar*	*juice of* 2 *large lemons*

Wipe the rhubarb, cut it into 1 in. lengths. Chop the figs. Put the sugar, rhubarb and figs into a large bowl, leave for 24 hours. Pour into a pan, bring to the boil, add the lemon juice, and cook until the rhubarb is tender and setting point is reached. Pot and cover.

Rhubarb and Orange Jam

1½ *lb. rhubarb*	1½ *lb. sugar*
4 *large oranges*	½ *pint water*

Wipe the rhubarb and cut it into 1 in. lengths. Wash and dry the oranges. Grate the peel, squeeze out the juice, scoop out any pulp. Put pips and pith in a muslin bag and put them in a bowl with the water, rhubarb, juice, peel and any pulp. Leave overnight. The next day put the mixture into the preserving pan, bring to the boil, simmer for 20 minutes. Remove pips and pith. Add the sugar, stirring until it is dissolved, then boil until setting point is reached. Pot and cover.

Common Strawberry Jam
(a Victorian recipe)

4 *lb. strawberries*	*juice of* 2 *large lemons*
4 *lb. sugar*	

Wash, hull and drain the strawberries. Put them in a heavy pan. Add the sugar, heat slowly until it is dissolved, stirring frequently. Add the lemon juice and boil vigorously until setting point is reached. Remove scum if necessary. Let the jam cool until a skin forms, stir to distribute the fruit. Pot and cover.

Whole Strawberry Jam
(an unusual French recipe)

4 lb. strawberries (small, just-ripe ones are best)
4 lb. sugar
juice of 2 lemons

Hull and wash the strawberries, drain them well. Put them in a large bowl with layers of sugar between. Leave overnight. The next day put the strawberries, lemon juice and sugar in a heavy saucepan, bring to the boil, then boil for 5 minutes – no more, no less. Remove from heat, pour back into the bowl and leave overnight. The next day boil for 6 minutes, leave overnight again. The third day bring to the boil again, and boil for 7 minutes this time. Remove scum if necessary. Let the jam cool until a skin forms, then stir lightly to distribute the fruit. Pot and cover. This way of making the jam keeps in the true flavour of the strawberries.

Low Sugar Jams
(for diabetics and people on diets)

A fine-flavoured low sugar jam can be made, but it does not keep well, only for a few weeks. Fruit high in pectin should be chosen: black and red currants, gooseberries, tart apples, damsons or quinces. Make in the usual way but only use ¾ lb.

sugar to each 1 lb. of fruit. Test for setting point by cold saucer or flake test (see page 27). When setting point is reached, pour the jam at once into hot jars and seal immediately (see pages 28–9). If clip jars or screw top jars are used, the jam can be put in a pan (with a false bottom) of hot water and sterilised (see page 26). Give screwbands a $\frac{1}{4}$ turn in reverse. Let the water reach boiling point, then boil the jars for 5 minutes. Remove jars, tighten screw bands and test for hermetic seal when cold (see page 26).

FRUIT BUTTERS, CHEESES AND CURDS

FRUIT BUTTERS

These are quite like fruit cheeses, but less sugar is used in making them. The texture is softer and they are often spiced. They should be potted in small jars and hermetically sealed (see paraffin wax, page 29). They are usually spread on bread and butter. They can also be used in trifles and to fill a sandwich cake. As they contain little sugar they should be used reasonably quickly, as they do not keep well.

The fruit should be washed and cut up, put in a heavy pan, just covered with water and simmered slowly until softened. Liquidise and put through a sieve; or just rub through a sieve. Weigh the pulp and allow $\frac{1}{2}$–$\frac{3}{4}$ lb. of sugar (according to sweetness of fruit) to each 1 lb. Put the pulp back in the pan and add the sugar and spices, too, if used. Stir and cook until the sugar is dissolved. Continue to cook until smooth, creamy and thick.

FRUIT CHEESES

These were called cheeses because they often replaced the cheese course. They used to be potted in special moulds and turned out when required and served cut in thick slices. They were eaten with bread and butter and sometimes cream cheese. Unlike fruit butters, fruit cheeses improve with keeping. They take more sugar, usually 1 lb. sugar to each 1 lb. of fruit pulp. As they need a lot of fruit, only make them when there is a glut.

Prepare the fruit, add water and cook in a covered pan until the fruit has sotened. Liquidise and put through a sieve; or rub through a sieve. Weigh the purée and allow 1 lb. sugar to each 1 lb. Put the sugar in the pan with the purée, stir until dissolved, then cook very slowly (this may take from 45–60 minutes) until the 'cheese' is thick. Stir frequently to prevent burning. It is sufficiently cooked when it comes away from the sides of the pan and a line made with a wooden spoon along the bottom of the pan does not fill in. If you do not own any of the old-fashioned moulds, spoon the hot cheese into warm jars. Put on waxed discs at once (see page 29). Cover and store.

FRUIT CURDS

This is quite a different kind of preserve as eggs and butter, as well as sugar, are added to the fruit. It can be used in many different ways; as a cake filling, for example, or for lemon curd tarts or orange curd puffs.

Apple Butter

Unless you use sharp, full-flavoured apples this really needs to have spices added; if not, it is rather insipid. If you have access to crab apples, they make a flavourful butter.

cider vinegar or water, to cover
spices (such as cinnamon, cloves, allspice, ginger) to taste

¾ lb. sugar to each 1 lb. pulp
grated lemon rind if liked

Wash the apples and cut them up small. Put them in a heavy pan, just cover them with cider vinegar or water, add the spices to taste. Simmer until the apples have softened. Rub through a sieve, or put through a vegetable mill, or liquidise and sieve. Weigh the purée and allow ¾ lb. sugar to each 1 lb. Put it back in the pan, add the sugar and stir until it is dissolved. Cook gently until thick and free of any excess liquid; stir frequently. Pour into warm pots, put a waxed disc on top, cover and store in a cool dry cupboard.

Damson Cheese

damsons
water to cover

1 lb. sugar to each 1 lb purée

Wash the damsons, remove any stalks. Put them in a heavy pan, just cover with water, put the lid on the pan. Simmer until the fruit is quite soft. Remove the stones, then liquidise and sieve, or rub the fruit through a sieve. Weigh the purée, allow 1 lb. sugar to each 1 lb. Put the purée in the pan, add the sugar, stir until dissolved. Cook gently until really thick, stirring frequently. When the mixture is very stiff, make a line on the bottom of the saucepan with a wooden spoon; if it does not fill in, the 'cheese' is sufficiently cooked. Spoon it into warm jars, put a waxed disc on top, cover and store in a cool, dry cupboard.

Lemon Curd

As this does not keep well, only make small quantities at a time. You will get about 2 lb. from the following.

4 large lemons
1 lb. caster sugar
6 oz. unsalted butter
4 large new-laid eggs

Wash the lemons, grate the rind, squeeze and strain the juice. Put the grated lemon rind, lemon juice, butter and sugar into the top of a double saucepan or into a basin fitting over a saucepan of boiling water. Heat gently, and let the sugar dissolve slowly, stirring from time to time. Beat the eggs lightly, strain them, then add them slowly to the butter-sugar mixture. Stir and cook until the mixture begins to thicken; do not let it boil or it may curdle. When it thickens, remove from the heat (as it cools it becomes even thicker). Pot in small jars, put waxed disc on top, smooth with the finger. Cover when cold.

Orange Curd

3 large, thin-skinned oranges
juice of 1 large lemon
¾ lb. caster sugar
6 oz. unsalted butter
4 large new-laid eggs

Wipe the oranges, grate the rind. Squeeze and strain the juice from the oranges and lemon. Put the butter in a double saucepan or basin over boiling water (as above), let it melt, then add the rind, juices and sugar, and stir until the sugar is dissolved. Beat the eggs lightly, strain them and add slowly to the orange-butter mixture. Stir until it thickens. Pot in small jars and cover. The lemon is added to sharpen the flavour, otherwise the orange can be rather sickly.

Quince Cheese

ripe quinces
water to cover
1 *lb. sugar to each* 1 *lb. purée*

Wipe the fuzz off the quinces, then cut them up small. There is no need to peel them or to remove the cores. Put the fruit in a heavy pan, just cover with water, put the lid on and simmer until the fruit is quite soft. Liquidise and sieve the purée, or rub it through a sieve, or put it through a vegetable mill. Weigh the purée, allow 1 lb. sugar to each 1 lb. Put the purée in the pan, add the sugar, heat and stir until it is dissolved. Cook gently until the mixture is stiff and there is no liquid left. Stir frequently. Make a line across the bottom of the pan with a wooden spoon; if it does not fill in, the 'cheese' is sufficiently cooked. Spoon it into warm jars, put a waxed disc on top, cover and store in a cool dry cupboard.

SAVOURY RECIPES USING JAM

Braised Lamb Chops

This is an attractive way to cook chops that you suspect may be tough.

1 lean chump chop per person. For 4 chops allow:

4–6 *skinned and chopped ripe tomatoes*
2 *tablespoons Morello jam (see page 39)*
freshly ground pepper and salt to taste
1 *teaspoon Worcestershire sauce*
2 *teaspoons dried mint (see page 192)*
fat for frying

Brown the chops on both sides in a very little fat. Pour off any excess fat or transfer the chops to another pan. Add the tomatoes, jam, pepper and salt, Worcestershire sauce and mint. Press the tomatoes with a wooden spoon. Put the lid on the pan and cook the meat gently for 15–20 minutes. Remove chops and keep hot while you correct the seasoning of the sauce. Serve the chops with the sauce poured over them and accompanied by runner or French beans.

Gooseberry Sauce

Heat the required amount of gooseberry (or gooseberry and elderflower) jam (see page 42), stir in a large tablespoon of butter and ¼ teaspoon of grated nutmeg. Serve with mackerel or roast pork.

Minced Ham with Cherry Sauce

Serves 4–6

1 *lb. minced cooked ham*
½ *lb. minced cooked pork*
3 *tablespoons fine white breadcrumbs*
1 *tablespoon finely chopped onion*
1 *tablespoon chopped parsley*
½ *teaspoon powdered sage*
1 *teaspoon sugar*
1 *gill milk*
2 *slightly beaten eggs*
1 *teaspoon dry mustard*
1 *teaspoon lemon juice*
plenty of freshly ground pepper

JAMS, FRUIT BUTTERS, CHEESES AND CURDS

Mix all the ingredients thoroughly together, press them into a greased 9 in. ring mould. Bake at 350°F. for 1 hour.

FOR THE CHERRY SAUCE

½ lb. jar cherry jam (see page 38)
1½ tablespoons cornflour (diluted with cold water)
grated lemon rind
freshly ground pepper
a few drops of Worcestershire sauce
hot water

Put the jam in a saucepan, add enough hot water to make 1 pint, stir to mix, Add the diluted cornflour, stir and cook until it thickens. Add grated lemon rind, pepper and Worcestershire sauce to taste.

Unmould the ring on to a serving dish. Fill the centre with a mixture of young vegetables: peas, carrots and new potatoes. Serve with the cherry sauce.

Partridges with Cherry Sauce

1 partridge per person *butter for frying*

TO STUFF 4 PARTRIDGE

3 petit Suisses
chopped giblets
4 oz. tin of liver pâté
pepper and salt
2 tablespoons cherry jam, preferably Morello (see page 39)

FOR THE CHERRY SAUCE

10 fluid oz. double cream
3 tablespoons cherry jam
1 tablespoon sherry
pepper and salt to taste

FOR THE CANAPÉS

4 *slices of white bread, crusts removed*

butter for frying

Brown the birds in hot butter. Pound the petit Suisses and the partridge giblets together. Mix in the liver pâté and cherry jam, season highly. Put a little of the stuffing in each bird, save some to spread on the fried bread. Sew up the partridges so that the stuffing cannot fall out. Put the birds in a heavy fireproof dish. Mix together the cream, sherry, cherry jam, pepper and salt, for the sauce. Pour it round them. Cook gently in a moderate oven (350°F.) for 30 minutes, or until the birds are tender. Make sure the sauce does not dry up; add more cream and cherry jam if necessary. When the partridges are cooked, fry the slices of bread in butter. Spread the rest of the stuffing on the fried bread. Lay a partridge on each slice, pour the sauce over, and serve with sauté potatoes and petit pois.

SWEET RECIPES USING JAM

Banana Trifle

Serves 4

4–5 *stale individual sponge cakes*
4 *bananas*
1 *tablespoon lemon juice*
3 *tablespoons strawberry or mulberry jam (see pages 49 & 44)*

thick custard
glacé cherries and desiccated coconut to decorate

JAMS, FRUIT BUTTERS, CHEESES AND CURDS

FOR THE CUSTARD

¾ pint milk
a sliver of lemon or orange peel
1½ oz. flour
4 egg yolks
1–1½ oz. caster sugar

Scald the milk, having added the lemon or orange peel. Put the flour, egg yolks and sugar into a basin. Beat until very light. Add the milk (remove the peel), beating continuously. Pour the custard into a double saucepan, or cook it in the basin over a saucepan of hot water. Cook slowly until it thickens and coats the back of the spoon. A line made on the back of the spoon should not close in if the custard is sufficiently thick.

TO ASSEMBLE THE TRIFLE

Split the sponge cakes in half. Peel the bananas, mash them with the lemon juice, beat in the jam. Spread the bottom half of the sponge cakes with this mixture, press the top half on. Arrange the filled sponge cakes in a shallow dish. Pour the custard on top. Chill. Serve sprinkled with the coconut and decorated with the glacé cherries.

Bread and Butter Fritters

Serves 4

8 slices of bread (crusts removed) spread with butter
greengage jam (see page 43)
coating batter
caster sugar
pure lard for frying (it should be at least 1 in. deep)

FOR THE COATING BATTER

4 oz. *plain flour*
pinch of salt

1 *tablespoon olive oil*
about 1 *gill warm water*

Sift flour and salt together. Mix in the oil, then add enough water until the mixture can be beaten. Beat thoroughly, then add more of the water until you have a thickish batter. It must be thick enough to stay on the bread. Leave 30 minutes before using. Spread half the slices of bread and butter with jam, cover with the other slices, press well together. Cut them into strips or triangles, dip them in the batter and fry until nicely brown. The fat mut be really hot so that the batter is sealed quickly. A simple test to see if the fat is hot enough is to heat it slowly, then put an inch cube of stale bread in it; if the fat is the right temperature, it should brown in 40 seconds.

As soon as the fritters are brown, drain them and sprinkle with caster sugar. Serve hot.

Cream Cheese Bar-le-Duc

Serves 3–4

6 oz. *unsalted cream cheese*
4 *tablespoons thick cream*

4 *tablespoons Bar-le-Duc jam*
(*see page* 36)

Mix the cream cheese and cream together until smooth. Fold in the jam. Serve chilled, with sponge fingers.

Croûtes Aux Cerises

Serves 6

1 *lb. jar of cherry jam (see page* 38)
1 *wineglass of red wine*
2 *strips of finely pared lemon peel*
12 *rounds of bread (crusts removed)*
butter for frying

Heat the jam slowly, with the wine and lemon peel. Fry the bread in hot butter. Pile some of the cherry mixture on top of each slice. Serve hot.

Curd or Jam Puffs

8 *oz. puff pastry (deep-frozen or see Appendix, page* 219)
Lemon or orange curd, or jam, for the filling
Beaten egg

Roll out the pastry to about $\frac{1}{8}$ in. thick. With a $2\frac{1}{2}$ in. – 3 in. cutter stamp out rounds. With a smaller cutter ($1\frac{1}{4}$ in. – $1\frac{1}{2}$ in.) mark the lids, but do not cut deeply. Moisten a baking tray with water, put the cases on and leave them in a cool place for 10 minutes. Brush over with beaten egg. Bake in a very hot oven (450°F) for 10–15 minutes, They should be brown and have risen three times their original size. Remove from the oven and with a small, sharp-pointed knife carefully remove the lid. Scoop out any soft and too lightly cooked paste from the case. When cool fill with curd or jam.

Guards' Pudding

4 oz. butter
4 oz. Barbados sugar
3 tablespoons raspberry jam (see page 47)
2 beaten eggs
4 oz. soft white breadcrumbs
½ teaspoon bicarbonate of soda dissolved in 1 dessertspoon warm water

Cream butter and sugar together until light in texture. Add the jam, beaten eggs, breadcrumbs and bicarbonate of soda. Mix thoroughly. Put the mixture into a buttered pudding basin and cover with foil. Steam for 2–2½ hours. Serve with hot raspberry sauce.

FOR THE SAUCE

4–6 tablespoons sieved raspberry jam
a nob of butter
good squeeze of lemon juice

Stir and heat all the ingredients together until they are smooth.

Jam Beignets

8 oz. shortcrust pastry (deep frozen or see Appendix, page 220)
any-flavoured jam or jelly
lightly beaten egg
caster sugar
oil for deep frying

Roll the pastry thinly into a rectangle. Divide it in half. Brush one half over with beaten egg, then lay blobs or jam or jelly at intervals. Put the other piece of pastry on top. Press well between the blobs and all round the edges. Brush over with egg. Cut into small squares. Fry in hot oil until the pastry is lightly brown. Serve with caster sugar sifted over them.

Jam Turnovers

shortcrust or puff pastry (deep frozen or see Appendix, pages 219, 220)
lightly beaten egg
caster sugar
any-flavoured jam

Roll the pastry out rather thinly. Stamp out rounds about 4 in. diameter. Put a little jam in the centre of each round. Wet the edges all round with water. Fold in half, flute round the edges with the back of a knife, brush over with beaten egg and sprinkle with caster sugar. Arrange the turnovers on a baking sheet and bake in a hot oven (400°F if using shortcrust pastry, 425°F for puff pastry) for about 20 minutes. The pastry should be lightly browned.

Lemon Curd and Apple Pie

$1\frac{1}{2}$ *lb. sweetened apple purée flavoured with lemon rind*
lemon curd (see page 54)
8–10 *finely crushed ginger biscuits*
3 *stiffly beaten egg whites*
3 *oz. caster sugar*

Put layers of apple purée, biscuit crumbs and lemon curd in a glass fireproof dish, ending with a layer of crumbs. Fold the sugar into the egg whites, pile on top of the pie, dredge with caster sugar. Put it in the oven at 310°F to set and lightly brown the meringue.

Mirlitons
(Macaroon Tarts)

For 14–16 small tarts

4 oz. *pâté sucrée* or shortcrust pastry (see *Appendix*, pages 219, 220)
apricot jam (see page 35)
2 egg whites
3½ oz. *caster sugar*
2½ oz. *ground almonds*
a few drops of almond essence
1 *teaspoon lemon juice*
icing sugar

Line patty pans with the pastry. Prick the base, spread with apricot jam. Beat the egg whites until stiff, fold in the sugar, ground almonds, almond essence and lemon juice. Put this almond mixture on top of the jam. Dredge with icing sugar. Bake at 380°F for 20–25 minutes.

Normandy Pudding

Serves 4–6

6–8 *plain sponge cakes*
1 *lb. peeled, cored and thinly sliced apples*
2–3 *oz. butter*
2 *liqueur glasses of Calvados or white wine*
1 *oz. sugar or to taste*
10 *fluid oz. double cream*
4–6 *tablespoons apricot jam (see page 35)*

Split the sponge cakes in half, arrange them in a fireproof dish. Mix together the Calvados, or white wine, sugar and cream. Pour half this mixture on to the cakes. Leave to soak for 30 minutes. Cook the apples in hot butter until they soften but do not break up. Arrange them on top of the sponge cakes. Spread thickly with apricot jam. Pour the rest of the cream, Calvados and sugar mixture over the pudding. Bake in a hot oven (425°F) for 5 minutes. Serve hot.

Poor Man's Baked Omelette

Serves 4

4 eggs
2 teaspoons caster sugar
3 oz. fine white breadcrumbs soaked in ½ gill milk
3–4 tablespoons blackberry and apple jam (see page 37)
1 oz. butter

Separate the eggs. Beat the yolks and the sugar until they are very light. Mix in the soaked breadcrumbs. Beat the egg whites until they are stiff but not dry. Fold them into the egg and bread mixture. Melt the butter in a shallow fireproof dish. Pour in half the mixture, put the jam on top, then the rest of the mixture. Bake at 325°F for 20–25 minutes. The omelette should be well risen and brown on top.

Raspberry Buns

6 oz. plain flour
6 oz. ground rice
1 teaspoon baking powder
4 oz. butter
4 oz. sugar
2 eggs
a little milk
raspberry jam (see page 47)

FOR THE TOPPING

a little beaten egg
24 sugar cubes coarsely crushed

Sieve the flour, ground rice and baking powder into a bowl. Rub the butter in with the finger tips. Mix in the sugar. Beat the eggs, add them and enough milk to make a stiff dough. Divide the mixture into small pieces (about 15), roll each piece into a ball. Make a deep indentation in each bun and put in some jam. Close the hole so that the jam is completely enclosed. Flatten the top, brush over with beaten egg and sprinkle the buns with the coarsely crushed sugar. Bake at 425°F for 10–15 minutes at the top of the oven.

Raspberry Custard Ice

Jam-flavoured frozen custards are especially good when home made jam is used. Switch the refrigerator to coldest temperature 30 minutes before freezing the ice cream.

1 pint custard (see below)
1 tablespoon lemon juice
½ lb. raspberry or other jam

a few drops of vegetable colouring if liked

CUSTARD FOR ICE CREAM

1 pint milk
3–4 eggs according to size

4 oz. sugar
a few drops of vanilla essence

Separate the eggs. Beat egg yolks and sugar together until light. Heat milk until nearly boiling, add it to the egg yolks and sugar. Pour back into the saucepan, cook over a low heat, stirring until mixture thickens and coats the back of the spoon. Do not let it boil or the eggs may curdle. Stir in the jam, essence, lemon juice, colouring if liked. Let it cool, stirring occasionally. Beat the egg whites stiffly, fold them in. Put the mixture into freezing trays, chill, then freeze.

Raspberry Noyau

You will need a sugar thermometer to make this.

14 oz. granulated sugar
1 gill water
3 oz. glucose
3 oz. raspberry jam (see page 47)
1 dessertspoon lemon juice
3 oz. chopped and roasted blanched almonds
rice paper (this is not easy to find in the shops; in London Selfridges stock it)

Put the sugar and water in a heavy pan, stir until dissolved over a low heat. Add the glucose and boil to 244°F, Hard Ball Stage (see page 15). Pour the mixture into a bowl. Leave until it has cooled; it should be just warm. Sieve the jam, add it and the lemon juice to the sugar. Stir vigorously until it looks creamy, then add the almonds. Line a shallow tin (about 6 in. × 4 in. × ½ in.) with rice paper. Spoon the mixture into the tin, level it, put another piece of rice paper on top. Leave overnight. Cut into small squares and wrap up in waxed paper.

Rose Petal Cake

8 oz. self-raising flour
8 oz. butter
8 oz. caster sugar
4 eggs
rose petal jam (see page 48)
1 teaspoonful rosewater (available from chemists)
pink icing
crystallised rose petals or other flowers

Cream the butter and sugar together until light and soft. Sieve the flour. Well beat the eggs. Add some of the beaten egg to the creamed mixture. Add a little flour, folding in carefully.

Continue adding egg and then flour and mixing thoroughly. Butter and lightly flour two 8 in. sandwich tins. Fill them equally with the cake mixture; hollow the centre a little so that they rise evenly. Bake in a hot oven (450°F), 20–25 minutes. Press gently with a finger, if there is no mark left they are cooked. Remove from tins, cool on a cake rack. When cold, spread one half plentifully with rose petal jam, then put the other half on top. Cover with palest pink icing and decorate with crystallised rose petals.

FOR THE ICING

6 *oz. sieved icing sugar*   *pink vegetable colouring*
2–3 *tablespoons rosewater*

Add the rosewater gradually to the icing sugar, beating well until you get a soft spreading icing. Add very little colouring to get the faintest of blush pinks. Smooth the icing on top of the cake with a warm palette knife. Decorate attractively.

Rouleau Rouennais
(Rouen Rolypoly)

8 *oz. shortcrust pastry (deep   Normandy apple conserve (see
  frozen or see Appendix, page   page* 35)
  220)

Roll out the pastry into an oblong shape and about $\frac{1}{4}$ in. thick. Cover it plentifully with the Normandy apple conserve. Moisten the edges with water. Roll up lightly. Press the edges well together to seal them. Put it on a well greased baking tin. Bake in the middle of a hot oven (425°F) for 30–35 minutes.

Look at it after 15 minutes; if it is getting too brown reduce the heat and cover with a piece of greaseproof paper. Serve hot or cold.

Witches' Froth

4 egg whites
4 heaped tablespoons icing sugar
4 heaped tablespoons mulberry or cherry jam (see pages 44 & 38)

Beat the egg whites until stiff. Add the sugar, beating it in. Gently fold in the jam. The mixture should be stiff and frothy. Chill and serve in glass bowls.

Blackcurrant Tea

Our grandmothers may not have known about vitamin C by name, but they did know how soothing and beneficial blackcurrant tea was for colds and sore throats. Put a heaping dessertspoon of blackcurrant jam in a mug or beaker, stir in boiling water. Sip it steaming hot in bed.

You can, of course, add more or less jam to taste.

Jellies

General Rules for Jelly Making
Pointers to Success

Bilberry Jelly
Blackberry Jelly
G-M's Spicy Hot Blackberry Jelly
Blackcurrant Jelly
Briar or Dog Rose Jelly
Crab Apple Jelly
Gooseberry Mint Jelly
Hedgerow Jelly
Hip and Haw Jelly
Minted Apple Jelly
Mulberry Jelly
New England Jelly
Quince Jelly
Redcurrant Jelly
Epicurean Redcurrant Jelly
Rose Geranium Jelly
Rowanberry Jelly
Violet Jelly

SAVOURY RECIPES USING JELLY

American Style Glazed Ham
Cumberland Sauce
Hare Pudding
Pork Chops with Quince Jelly
Pork with Pimientos and Quince Jelly
Rabbit Pie
Vance's Stuffed Kidneys

SWEET RECIPES USING JELLY

French Apple Tart
German Obstorte (Fruit Salad Tart)
Peach Fritters
Strawberry Tart

JELLIES

GENERAL RULES FOR JELLY MAKING

Jam and jelly making are similar; they both need pectin, acid and sugar in the correct proportion to get a firm set.

Fruit Wild fruits, such as early blackberries, sloes, elderberries, bilberries, crab apples, are suitable. Red, black and white currants, gooseberries, quinces and tart apples are excellent. The fruit should be just ripe and used as soon as possible after it has been picked. As only the strained juice is used, fruit that is not quite perfect is all right. Any bruised or specked pieces should be cut away.

Strawberries, raspberries and peaches are generally too low in pectin to be successful. A combination of fruits, low and high in pectin, can be cooked together. Strawberry and gooseberry, raspberry and redcurrant, blackberry and apple are examples. If you do not want to blend a low pectin fruit, use a pectin booster (see page 24).

Wash the fruit, remove any bruised or spoiled parts. Do not peel it or remove stems from currants. The amount of water added when cooking the fruit depends on juiciness and type.

First Extract Put the fruit and water in a heavy pan. Simmer, without sugar, until it has softened. Press the fruit with a wooden spoon as it cooks, to help the juice run. Simmer for 30–60 minutes until it has completely broken down. The pectin and acid must be released and dissolved in the water in order to

JELLIES

make a strong jelly. Strain the fruit in a jelly bag for a few hours, or overnight, but do not leave it longer than 24 hours.

Second Extract If you have tested that the fruit is rich in pectin (see page 26) or if the juice looks viscous, which means it has a high gelling potential, you can make a second extract.

After the preliminary cooking of the fruit, strain it for 30 minutes only. Remove the pulp carefully from the jelly bag, put it in the pan, add half the amount of water originally used. Stir to break up the pulp. Simmer it gently for 30–40 minutes. Strain it again through the jelly bag for at least 2–3 hours. (There is no need to wash the jelly bag between the two operations.) You can either combine the two extracts of juice to make one batch of jelly or make two different lots using the first and second extracts separately.

Making the Jelly Measure the strained juice into the pan, bring it to the boil, add the required amount of sugar, usually 1 lb. sugar to 1 pint of juice (see individual recipes). Stir until the sugar is dissolved, then boil vigorously.

It is important to use the right quantity of sugar so that the jelly will set without having to be cooked for too long. Overcooking causes too great a concentration of pectin, and excess pectin makes the jelly elastic and rubbery so that it will not spread easily. It also causes the sugar to caramelise, which spoils both colour and flavour. The colour should be bright and clear and the flavour distinct and identifiable. A poor-coloured jelly may be caused by using fruit that is pale, or by too slow cooking. When turned out the jelly should keep its shape and yet still 'wriggle like a jelly on a plate'.

When the jelly begins to thicken, start testing for setting point. This is best done with a sugar thermometer, which should register 220°F, indicating a sugar concentration of 60 – 65 per cent. If you do not have a thermometer, test by the flake test (see page 27).

Potting As soon as setting point is reached, turn off the heat. Remove any scum. Pour the liquid slowly into warm jars. If it is allowed to cool much before pouring, it will begin to set and the texture be spoilt. Once the jars are filled, they should not be moved until they are cold as this too may disturb the setting. Once gelation has begun, if the gel structure is then disrupted by movement the jelly is weakened. Put waxed discs on at once; smooth gently with the finger to exclude all air – this is most important as air can be the cause of mould formation. Cover at once or leave until quite cold before covering. For preference use small pots because once they are opened and left they may 'weep' (see page 20) and become runny. This is called syneresis (see page 226).

POINTERS TO SUCCESS

- Use freshly picked, just-ripe fruit.

- Simmer the fruit gently until it is well broken up and soft.

- Strain for at least 2–3 hours or overnight, but no longer.

- Do not squeeze the jelly bag, this could make the jelly cloudy. Shift the balance of the pulp so that more juice runs out.

- As soon as the sugar is dissolved, boil rapidly until the jelly thickens and setting point is reached.

- Do not over-boil; this spoils colour and flavour.

- Immediately setting point is reached, remove scum and pour the jelly slowly into jars.

- As soon as the pot is full, smooth on waxed disc to exclude air.

- Cover at once or leave until quite cold.

- Make certain that the fruit is high enough in pectin to get a good set. If not, add a pectin booster (see page 24).

Bilberry Jelly

If you find bilberries in the country and have the patience to pick them they make an excellent jelly. You will need about 4 lb. to get 1 pint of juice.

1½ lb. sugar to 1 pint juice

Wash the bilberries. Put them in the pan over a low heat. Press them with a wooden spoon as they are cooking, to help the juice run. Bring to the boil and cook gently until the fruit is softened. Strain through a jelly bag overnight. Measure the juice, weigh out the required amount of sugar. Heat the juice, add the sugar, stir until dissolved. Boil vigorously until setting point is reached. Pot and cover.

This jelly goes well with all kinds of game.

Blackberry Jelly

3–4 lb. blackberries
juice of 2 lemons
¾ pint water
1 lb. sugar to each 1 pint juice

Pick over the fruit and wash it. Put it in a pan, add the water and lemon juice. Cook slowly until the blackberries have softened. Press them as they are cooking with a wooden spoon, to help extract the juice. Strain through a jelly bag overnight. The next day measure the juice, add the required amount of sugar and stir over a low heat until it is dissolved. Boil vigorously until setting point is reached. Pot and cover.

G.-M's Spicy Hot Blackberry Jelly

Add 1 chopped chilli to the above quantities when the blackberries are first cooked. Proceed in the same way as above.

This is an unusual spicy jelly which can be served with hot or cold game dishes or it can be added to stews and casseroles. It is very hot.

Blackcurrant Jelly

3 lb. blackcurrants
1½ pints water
1 lb. sugar to each 1 pint juice

Wash the fruit, but there is no need to remove stalks. Put it in the pan, add the water, bring to the boil, then simmer until the skins are really soft. This is important because once the sugar is added they will not soften any more. Press with a wooden spoon as they are cooking, to extract all the juice. Strain through a jelly bag overnight. Measure the juice and allow 1 lb. sugar to each 1 pint. Heat the juice, add the sugar, stir until dissolved. Bring to the boil and boil vigorously until setting point is reached. Pot and cover.

Briar or Dog Rose Jelly

Get up early one June morning and pick briar roses until you have about half a pound; then capture their fragrance, in a jelly for winter days.

8 *oz. briar rose petals*	1 *gill water*
1 *lb. redcurrants*	1 *lb. sugar to* 1 *pint juice*

Pick over the petals, choose the best ones, wash if necessary. Put them in a pan, just cover with water and cook gently for 15 minutes. Strain them. Wash the redcurrants, add 1 gill of water and cook them until the fruit has softened. Put them in a scalded piece of muslin and squeeze out all the juice. Measure the liquid from the rose petals and the redcurrants. Add the required amount of sugar, stir until the sugar is dissolved. Boil vigorously until setting point is reached. Skim if necessary. Pot in miniature jars. Cover. If you do not get enough juice from the rose petals and redcurrants, you can make up the amount by adding half lemon juice and water.

This can be used instead of red rose petal conserve for the rose petal cake (see page 67) or a little can be eaten with thick cream.

Crab Apple Jelly

3 *lb. crab apples*	*cloves, ginger or cinnamon for additional flavour if liked*
water to cover	
2 *tablespoons lemon juice*	1 *lb. sugar to each* 1 *pint juice*

Choose just-ripe crab apples. Wash them well, remove stalks, cut the crab apples in half. Put them in a pan, just cover with water, add spices if being used. Simmer until the fruit is soft. Strain overnight. Measure juice, add required amount of sugar, stir to dissolve, add lemon juice, boil vigorously until setting point is reached. Pot and cover.

Serve instead of the traditional cranberry sauce with roast turkey, or with roast mutton.

Gooseberry Mint Jelly

4 lb. unripe green gooseberries
water
1 lb. sugar to each 1 pint juice
a few mint stalks
a large handful of freshly chopped mint
green vegetable colouring if liked

Wash the gooseberries, put them in a pan, just cover with water. Add the mint stalks. Bring slowly to the boil, cook until the skins have softened. Strain overnight in a jelly bag. Measure the juice, add the required amount of sugar, stir until dissolved. Add the chopped mint, boil gently for about 10 minutes, then test for setting point. Add green colouring if being used. Pot and cover.

This can be served with hot or cold roast lamb.

Hedgerow Jelly

This is a blend of wild blackberries, sloes and elderberries. I find it sets very well and is a wonderful deep rich red.

4 lb. blackberries
½ lb. sloes
½ lb. elderberries
2 tablespoons lemon juice
1 pint water
allow 1 lb. sugar to each 1 pint juice

Wash and pick over the fruit, strip the elderberries from their stems. Put the fruit in the pan, cover with water, bring to the boil. Squash the fruit with a wooden spoon as it is cooking to extract all the juice. Simmer slowly until fruit has softened. Strain through a jelly bag overnight. Measure the juice, heat it, add the sugar, stir until it is dissolved. Bring to the boil, add the lemon juice and boil vigorously until setting point is reached. Pot and cover.

Hip and Haw Jelly

This jelly has a strange flavour which goes well with all kinds of furred or feathered game.

equal quantity of hips and haws water

1 lb. sugar and juice of ½ lemon to each 1 pint juice

Wash the hips and haws thoroughly. Put them in a pan, cover with cold water. Bring to the boil and simmer gently until the berries are soft. Strain overnight through a jelly bag. The juice does not look attractive, a rather dull brown, but when it is boiled with the sugar it changes to a dark red. Measure the juice into the pan, add the required amount of sugar and lemon juice. Stir until the sugar is dissolved, then boil quickly until setting point is reached. Pot and cover.

Minted Apple Jelly

3 lbs. just ripe, sharp green apples
a bunch of washed, fresh young mint including stems
1 pint white vinegar

1 lb. sugar to each pint liquid
3-4 tablespoons finely chopped fresh mint
a few drops of green vegetable colouring

Wash the apples, cut them up roughly, do not remove cores or pips. Put the apples in a heavy pan, add the water and the bunch of mint. Simmer until the apples are quite soft. Add the vinegar, boil for 5–6 minutes. Strain through a jelly cloth overnight. Measure the liquid, add the required amount of sugar. Bring to the boil slowly, stirring until the sugar is dissolved. Add the chopped mint and colouring. Boil vigorously until setting point is reached. Skim if necessary. Let the jelly cool until a skin begins to form on top, then stir gently to distribute the chopped mint evenly. Pour into small, hot jars, put on waxed discs at once, cover when cold.

This jelly is excellent with roast lamb.

Mulberry Jelly

3 lb. slightly under-ripe mulberries *1 lb. sugar to each 1 pint juice*
1 pint water *1 tablespoon lemon juice*

Pick over the mulberries, wash, remove stalks. Put the fruit in the pan and cover with the water. Cook slowly until softened. Strain overnight in a jelly bag. Measure the juice, put it in the pan, add the required amount of sugar. Heat and stir until the sugar is dissolved, add the lemon juice. Bring to the boil and cook until setting point is reached. Pot and cover.

This rather tart jelly goes well with game, roast turkey, mutton or lamb.

New England Jelly

4 lb. sharp apples *water*
2 lb. quinces *1 lb. sugar for each 1 pint juice*
4 oz. cranberries (fresh or deep frozen)

Wash and cut up the apples and quinces. Do not peel or core them. Put them in the pan, add the cranberries, just cover with water. Cook slowly until all the fruit is soft. Strain overnight in a jelly bag. Measure the juice and to each 1 pint allow 1 lb. sugar. Heat the juice, add the sugar, stir until it is dissolved, then boil rapidly until setting point is reached. Pot and cover.

This jelly goes very well with all game, especially venison, and with poultry, especially turkey.

Quince Jelly

4 *lb. under-ripe quinces*
6 *pints water*
2 *tablespoons lemon juice*
1 *lb. sugar to each* 1 *pint juice*

Wipe the quinces thoroughly to remove the fuzz. Cut them up, but do not core or peel them. Put them in the pan, add the water. As the quinces are hard, quite a lot of water is added but as they need to cook for about 1 hour a fair amount is lost by evaporation. When the quinces have softened, put them in a jelly bag and leave to drip overnight. Measure the juice, allow 1 lb. sugar to each 1 pint of juice. Heat the juice, add the sugar and lemon juice, stir until dissolved. Boil vigorously until setting point is reached. Pot and cover.

Redcurrant Jelly

3 *lb. redcurrants*
1½ *pints water*
1 *lb. sugar to each* 1 *pint juice*

Wash the fruit, put it in a pan, add water, bring to the boil, then simmer gently until the skins are really soft. Press with a wooden spoon while the fruit is cooking, to extract all the juice. Strain overnight in a jelly bag. Measure the juice and allow 1 lb. sugar to each 1 pint. Heat the juice, add the sugar, stir until it is dissolved. Bring to the boil vigorously until setting point is reached. Pot and cover.

Epicurean Redcurrant Jelly

This is a superlative jelly, with a fine flavour and texture. It is the pure unadulterated fruit juice, only sugar being added to sweeten and preserve it. Ideal for serving with game, and roast mutton when you can get it. The yield is small and from 6 lb. of fruit you will only get about 3 lb. of jelly.

6 lb. redcurrants $1\frac{1}{4}$ *lb. sugar to each 1 pint juice*

Wash the currants and remove any leaves. There is no need to stalk them, as the pulp is strained. Put them in the pan, let them cook very gently until they have softened and the juice runs freely. Press them with a wooden spoon from time to time, to help extract the juice. When they are really soft (and this may take 45 minutes at least), mash them and strain through a jelly bag overnight. Measure the juice, allow $1\frac{1}{4}$ lb. sugar to each 1 pint. Heat the juice slowly, add the sugar, stir until it is dissolved. Bring to the boil and boil for 1 minute. Skim if necessary. Pour at once into tiny warmed jars. This jelly solidifies quickly and once setting point has been reached it begins to set in the pan. Cover in the usual way.

Rose Geranium Jelly

$2\frac{1}{2}$ lb. crab apples or sharp apples *1 lb. sugar to each 1 pint fruit*
2 pints water *juice*
a handful of rose geranium leaves

JELLIES

Wash the fruit, cut it up roughly. Wash the leaves, put them in a pan with the apples, cover with the water and simmer until the fruit is quite soft and like a purée. Strain through a jelly bag overnight. The next day measure the juice, heat it in the pan, add the required amount of sugar and stir until it is dissolved, then boil vigorously until setting point is reached. Pot and cover.

This makes a pleasant filling for a sandwich cake.

Rowanberry Jelly

If you have a tree in the garden or are given some rowanberries you might like to try this. Only make a small amount as it has a very distinctive – and to some people unattractive – flavour.

2 lb. rowanberries
1 pint water
1 tablespoon lemon juice
1 lb. sugar to each 1 pint juice

Remove the berries from the stems, wash them well – it is amazing how dirty they usually are. Put them in the pan, cover with the water and lemon juice and cook until they are soft. Strain through a jelly bag overnight, add the sugar, stir until it is dissolved. Boil until setting point is reached. Pot and cover.

Only serve this jelly with strong-flavoured meats and game.

Violet Jelly

1 lb. tart apples
1 gill water
juice of half a large lemon
1 lb. sugar to each 1 pint of liquid
a generous handful of sweet-scented violet heads

Wipe the apples, quarter them. Do not peel or core. Add a gill of water to each pound, simmer until the apples are soft, strain through a jelly bag overnight. The next day measure the liquid, allow 1 lb. sugar to each 1 pint. Heat the liquid, add the sugar, stir until dissolved. Add the lemon juice, bring to the boil. Add the violets tied in muslin. Boil vigorously for 5 minutes or until setting point is reached. Remove scum if necessary. Remove violets. Pot and cover.

When I make this I never know what to do with it except to give it to friends as an oddity.

SAVOURY RECIPES USING JELLY

American Style Glazed Ham

5–6 *lb. middle gammon*
1 *gill white wine vinegar*
1 *gill pineapple juice*
2 *crushed bay leaves*

4 *oz. Barbados sugar*
6 *black peppercorns*
3–4 *cloves*
water

FOR THE GLAZE

1 *teaspoon dry mustard*
2 *tablespoons brown sugar*
6 *tablespoons redcurrant jelly (see page* 81*)*
6–8 *quartered glacé cherries*

10–12 *blanched and halved almonds*
an extra 3 *tablespoons redcurrant jelly mixed with* 2 *tablespoons white wine*

Soak the ham overnight unless you are using processed ham, when it is unnecessary. Put the ham in a saucepan, with the vinegar, pineapple juice, bay leaves, sugar, peppercorns and cloves, and add enough water to cover the ham. Bring slowly

JELLIES

to the boil and simmer gently. Allow 20–30 minutes per pound for smoked ham and 15–25 minutes per pound for processed ham. When the ham is cooked, remove from the saucepan. When it is cool enough to handle, remove the skin. Mix together the dry mustard and brown sugar, spread it over the ham. Put the ham in a greased baking dish, spread it all over with redcurrant jelly. Bake at 350°F for 20 minutes. Remove from oven. With a sharp knife make ¼ in. gashes to form 2 in. squares. Arrange the almonds and cherries attractively on top, Brush over with the extra redcurrant jelly and white wine. Bake for a further 15 minutes. Serve with boiled small new potatoes and a spinach purée.

Cumberland Sauce

the peel of 1 orange and 1 lemon
iuice of 1 orange
juice of ½ lemon
½ lb. jar of redcurrant jelly (see page 81)

1 gill port wine or medium sherry
good pinch cayenne pepper
freshly ground pepper
½ teaspoon Worcestershire sauce

Cut the orange and lemon peel into thin strips, boil them for 5 minutes to get rid of bitterness. Drain off the water. Heat the jelly slowly, add the fruit juices, strips of peel, port or sherry, cayenne pepper and pepper, and the Worcestershire sauce. Stir until all is well mixed. Serve hot or cold. There is no need to add any thickening, as the jelly stiffens when cold. 2 Seville oranges can be used instead of the orange and lemon juice, or 2 tablespoons of thin-cut marmalade. This sauce enhances many dishes – roast venison, duck, cold cuts such as ham, tongue and brawn are a few. If kept in a closed jar in the refrigerator or a cool cupboard, it keeps well for several weeks.

Hare Pudding

This old English pudding makes for compulsive eating on a cold and frosty day.

Serves 5–6

10 oz. suet crust (see Appendix, page 221)
1 small, young, jointed hare
seasoned flour
3–4 streaky bacon rashers, diced
1 chopped onion
2 chopped cloves of garlic
2 oz. sliced mushrooms
1 bay leaf
a sprinkling of thyme
pepper and salt
1 tablespoon crab apple jelly (see page 77)
1 teaspoon mushroom ketchup (see page 217)
3–4 tablespoons port wine

Grease a 2-pint pudding basin. Cut off a third of the suet crust for the lid. Roll out the large piece into a round to fit into the basin and about ¼ in. thick. Line the basin with it. Smooth out any creases. Dip the hare joints in the seasoned flour. Put half quantities of hare, onion, garlic, mushrooms and rashers into the basin. Add the bay leaf, some of the thyme, some pepper, and only a little salt because the mushroom ketchup is salty. Add the rest of the hare, onion, garlic, mushrooms and rashers, and a little more thyme and pepper. Mix together the jelly, ketchup and port wine and pour into the basin.

Roll out the rest of the pastry, damp the edges with water and put it on top of the pudding. Press the edges well together so that none of the aroma escapes. Cover with greased greaseproof paper, making a pleat in the centre so that the crust can rise, or cover the basin with aluminium foil. Fold the edges round the rim of the basin. Cut a long strip of foil about 10 in. wide, fold it in half, put the basin in the middle, lower it gently into a pan of boiling water on to an inverted saucer. The water should come about half-way up the basin. Put on the lid, leaving the ends of the foil protruding, as this makes for easy removal when the pudding is cooked. Simmer gently for 3 hours. If preferred, steam for 4–4½ hours. Serve with the following gravy.

GRAVY FOR HARE PUDDING

1 *gill water*
1 *gill port wine*
1 *tablespoon crab apple jelly (see page 77)*
1 *teaspoon mushroom ketchup (see page 217)*
1 *teaspoon tomato concentrate*
pepper and salt to taste

Heat and stir all the ingredients together. Serve on the side.

Pork Chops with Quince Jelly

1 chop per person. For each chop allow:

3 *tablespoons quince jelly or quince cheese (see pages 81, 55)*
1 *tablespoon liquid honey*
1 *tablespoon boiling water*
a scant teaspoon white wine vinegar
pepper and salt to taste
oil for frying

Brown the chops on both sides in the oil. Put them in a fireproof dish, season. Put the honey, jelly, boiling water and vinegar in the frying pan, stir and bring to the boil. Pour it over the chops, cover the dish and cook at 350°F for 45–60 minutes according to the thickness of the chops. Serve with the sauce poured round, a potato purée and French beans to accompany and extra jelly on the side.

Pork with Pimientos and Quince Jelly

Serves 4

1 *large chopped onion*	1¼–1½ *lb. pork fillet*
2 *chopped cloves garlic*	*fat for frying*
1 *sliced fresh or pickled pimiento (see page* 171)	

FOR THE SAUCE

5–6 *tablespoons quince jelly or quince jelly jam (see pages* 81, 46)	1 *teaspoon dry mustard*
1 *tablespoon brown sugar*	*salt to taste*
1 *tablespoon Worcestershire Sauce*	2 *teaspoons cornflour (diluted with cold water)*
2 *tablespoons vinegar from pickled pimientos (see page* 171)	3–4 *tablespoons hot water*

Fry the onion, garlic and pimiento for 3–4 minutes in hot fat. Cut the pork fillet into ½-in. thick slices. Put it in the pan with the vegetables and brown all over, then cook for about 10 minutes. Keep hot. Put the sugar, jelly, Worcestershire sauce, vinegar, mustard and hot water in a pan, heat and stir until the sugar is dissolved. Add the blended cornflour. Bring to the boil, stir until sauce thickens. Add salt to tast. Correct flavour. If a sharper taste is liked add more vinegar; if sweeter, add more sugar. Pour the sauce over the pork. Serve with plain boiled rice.

Rabbit Pie

Serves 6-8

1 *large jointed rabbit*	2 *tablespoons blackcurrant jelly*
seasoned flour	*(see page 76)*
2 *chopped onions*	*pepper and salt*
2 *oz. mushrooms*	1 *gill white wine*
8 *chipolatas*	1 *gill stock*
2 *quartered hard-boiled eggs*	*butter for frying*
8 *oz. diced pickled pork*	8 *oz. puff pastry (deep frozen*
pinch of powdered rosemary or thyme (see page 192)	*or see Appendix, page 219)*
	beaten egg for glazing

Coat the rabbit in seasoned flour. Soften the onions and mushrooms in hot butter. Brown the rabbit all over. Add white wine, stock, blackcurrant jelly (this gives the sauce an unusual flavour), rosemary or thyme, pepper and salt to taste. Bring to the boil. Fry the sausages. Arrange the rabbit, pickled pork, sausages and hard-boiled eggs in a pie dish. Pour in the liquid. Roll out the pastry to fit the pie dish. Line the edge of the dish with a strip of pastry, cover the pie with the rest of the pastry. Trim and flute the edges. Make two slits in the centre. Brush over with beaten egg to glaze. Cook in a hot oven (450°F) for 15 minutes. Reduce heat to 350°F and cook for $1\frac{1}{2}$–$1\frac{3}{4}$ hours longer. This pie can be served hot or cold with blackcurrant jelly on the side. A purée of turnip tops goes well with this dish.

Vance's Stuffed Kidneys

Allow 2-3 lamb's kidneys, according to size, per person.

8–12 *kidneys*

FOR THE STUFFING

4 *oz. butter*
plenty of chopped parsley
2 *oz. fine white breadcrumbs*
1 *tablespoon sherry or port*
pepper and salt to taste
1 *tablespoon bilberry jelly (see page* 75)
1 *completely chopped and crushed clove of garlic*
1 *minced shallot*
1 *dessertspoon banana and apple chutney (see page* 158)
1 *tablespoon Worcestershire sauce*
1 *teaspoon dry mustard*

Mix all the ingredients together until you have a rather moist stuffing. Add more sherry or port if necessary, or if too moist, add more breadcrumbs.

Split the kidneys from the rounded side towards the core, but do not separate them. Now remove the fine skin; this is more easily done once they are split. Take care not to cut the kidneys when removing it. Arrange plenty of stuffing on each kidney. Tie them up loosely with white thread. Arrange them in a well buttered shallow fireproof dish. Cook at 425°F for 10–12 minutes. Kidneys are far better under than over cooked. Remember to remove the white thread when they are cooked to your liking. Serve with watercress and perfectly cooked crisp chip potatoes to contrast texture.

SWEET RECIPES USING JELLY

French Apple Tart

This tart is filled with an apple purée, thinly sliced apples overlapping on top. The pastry case is partially cooked then filled with the purée and the uncooked apple slices arranged on the surface. Then it is put back in the oven and cooked until the pastry is brown and the apples done.

8 oz. *pâte sucrée (see Appendix, page* 219) *or shortcrust pastry (deep frozen or see Appendix, page* 220) *to make a* 10 *in. pastry case*

3 *lb. sharp cooking apples (such as Bramleys)*

1 *lb. eating apples (Cox's or Golden Delicious)*

2 *tablespoons quince jelly (see page* 81)

2–3 *oz. sugar or to taste*

pinch of ground cloves, cinnamon or grated lemon rind

quince or apricot glaze

Cut up the 3 lb. of apples, put them in a heavy pan and cook them with the lid on. Stir occasionally. When they are soft, liquidise them or put them through a vegetable mill. Put the purée back in the pan, add the quince jelly, sugar, spices or lemon rind. Stir and cook until the purée is very thick. Peel, core and slice the eating apples. Put them in a bowl and sprinkle them with lemon juice to prevent them discolouring.

Roll out the pastry $\frac{1}{8}$ in. thick to fit a 10 in. tin or flan ring (see Appendix, page 221). Pick the pastry up on the rolling pin, lay it over the tin, press it down lightly. Pass the rolling pin over the top to trim off the edges. With the thumbs push the pastry up ⅛ in. above the edge of the tin. With the back of a knife nick the pastry edge at equal intervals all round. Prick the base of the pastry all over. Line it with greased greaseproof paper, cover it with dry haricot beans. Bake at 375°F until the pastry is set (about 8–10 minutes). Remove from oven, take out paper and beans. Fill it with the apple purée, cover with the apple slices arranged in concentric circles. Bake at 375°F until the apples have softened and the edges are brown (this may take 25–30 minutes). Glaze with quince jelly (see page 94) or sieved apricot jam (see page 35). Serve just warm or cold.

German Obstorte
(Fruit Salad Tart)

The Germans are very fond of fruit salad tart and make it superbly. They use skinned and de-pipped black and white grapes, sliced banana (soaked in lemon juice to prevent discolouration), bottled peaches, apricots, pears and cherries. They arrange the drained fruit on a cooked pastry case, either in concentric rings or in segments of individual fruits. It is then glazed with light-coloured jelly (see page 94).

Peach Fritters

Allow 2–3 peach halves per person

well drained bottled or tinned peaches (see page 131)   *caster sugar and redcurrant jelly for topping (see page 81)*

JELLIES

FOR THE BATTER

2 eggs
6 oz. flour
1 teaspoon sugar
1 tablespoon olive oil

2 tablespoons brandy
cold water
oil for frying

Beat the eggs until they are quite light. Add the flour, sugar and olive oil, mix well. Add the brandy gradually and enough cold water to make a thinnish batter – the consistency of double cream. Beat until it is smooth. It must be thick enough to coat the fruit. Dip the fruit in the batter. Heat the oil in a deep pan until it is just below smoking hot – about 375°F. Put in 2–3 peach halves at a time. When the batter is golden brown, remove the peaches carefully, and drain. Keep hot while you fry the rest of them. Serve sprinkled with caster sugar and topped with redcurrant jelly.

Strawberry Tart

For a 10 in. tart

8 oz. pâte sucrée (see Appendix, page 219) or shortcrust pastry (deep frozen or see Appendix, page 220)

1 lightly beaten egg white
$1\frac{1}{4}$–$1\frac{1}{2}$ lb. fresh strawberries
redcurrant or crab apple glaze

Roll out the pastry to $\frac{1}{8}$ in. thick, and $1\frac{1}{2}$ in. larger than the tart pan or flan ring. (To line a flan ring see Appendix, page 221.) Prick the pastry base all over. Bake 'blind' (see Appendix, page 221). Hull the strawberries, wipe them, wash if necessary.

Arrange them attractively on the cooked case. If any of the strawberries are very big they can be halved and placed cut side down. Spoon or brush on the glaze.

Raspberry and red or black currant tarts can be made in this way.

TO MAKE THE GLAZE

½ *lb. redcurrant or crab apple*   1 *tablespoon lemon juice*
 jelly (*see pages* 81, 77)

Stir and dissolve the jelly and lemon juice in a small pan over a low heat. Let it cook until it has reduced slightly or the temperature is 228°F.

Marmalades

Introduction
Pointers to Success

Prototype Marmalade Recipe: Andalusian Orange Marmalade
Dark Chunky Marmalade
Family Marmalade
Four Fruit Marmalade
Grapefruit Marmalade
Green Tomato Marmalade
Orange Jelly Marmalade
Lemon Jelly Marmalade
West Indian Lime Marmalade
Pressure Cooker Marmalade

SAVOURY RECIPES USING MARMALADE

Glazed Sweet Potatoes
Boiled Pork with Orange Sauce
Orange Stuffed Pork Rolls
Wild Duck with Bigarade Sauce
Veal and Orange

SWEET RECIPES USING MARMALADE

Baked Pears with Marmalade Sauce
Marmalade Tart
Marronmarma Cream
Vermicelli Pudding

MARMALADES

INTRODUCTION

Originally the word 'marmalade' came from the Greek – 'honey apple'. In France it is the word used for a compôte of fruit, or for stewed apples and for some jams. In England it is almost always a conserve of citrus fruit. To the rest of the world bacon, egg and marmalade are the symbols of the British way of life. There are 365 breakfast days in our year in which to eat marmalade; apart from this it is very versatile and can be used for many savoury and sweet dishes, so do make a good batch.

Marmalade can be dark and tangy, chunky and coarse or a jelly with a few wafer-thin slices of peel suspended in it. The most popular is usually made with bitter Seville oranges; they have a clean, strong taste. The Seville orange season is a short one – from January to February, but the marmalade can be made out of season now, for large tins of prepared oranges are on sale in many shops.

Although this preserve contains sugar and fruit, like jam, there are some differences in the making. It should be made as soon as possible after the oranges are bought, for the pectin is high then, especially in the pith and pips which should always be used. Tie them loosely in a muslin bag and soak and simmer them with the fruit. The bag can be tied to the handle of the preserving pan for easy removal.

The fruit can be cut up by hand (oranges and lemons can be left in boiling water for 3 minutes, to soften the peel before slicing them); or minced, but this can cause a cloudy marmalade.

MARMALADES

If you have an electric mixer with attachments, the peel can be shredded with the high speed slicer and shredder. It can also be covered with some of the water in which it has been soaking and then chopped in a liquidiser, but only for a short time. You must experiment to get the cut you want.

Citrus peel is tough, so it should be soaked for 24–48 hours. Some schools of thought nowadays say this is unnecessary, but I find it preferable. After soaking, cook it until it is tender (this may take from 1½–2 hours) before sugar is added. The water in which the peel, pips and pith are soaked is used for cooking the peel.

Tastes vary considerably. Some people only like a chunky marmalade, others a medium cut, while many people who like the flavour but cannot digest the peel, prefer a jelly marmalade. The making of the different types is very similar, but the results are quite different.

The yield from few oranges is high. 1½ lb., or about 5–6 oranges, makes about 5 lb. marmalade.

POINTERS TO SUCCESS

- Citrus fruit should be well scrubbed before using.

- Always use any pith you remove and the pips, tied up loosely in a muslin bag, when fruit is soaked and cooked. They contain pectin.

- Always add lemon juice (except for lemon or lime marmalade). About 2 tablespoons to each 1 lb. of Seville oranges.

- Never add the sugar until the peel is really soft and quite a lot of the water has evaporated.

PRESERVING WITH SUGAR

- Once sugar is added and has dissolved, boil rapidly.

- As soon as setting point is reached, turn off the heat, remove scum. Leave the marmalade to cool for about 15 minutes or until a skin forms. Stir to distribute the peel. This prevents peel rising to the top of the jar.

- Read the prototype recipe – Andalusian Orange Marmalade – it contains in full detail the processes which are only briefly mentioned in the other recipes.

Prototype Marmalade Recipe: Andalusian Orange Marmalade

1½ lb. Seville oranges
4 pints water
juice of 1 large lemon

1 lb. sugar to each 1 pint of cooked fruit with its liquid

Wash the fruit thoroughly, especially round the stalk end – quite a lot of dirt collects there. Use a very sharp stainless steel knife and cut the oranges in half. Squeeze out the juice. Keep the pips. Cut up the peel by hand, mincer or electric shredder. If you do it by hand, put the cut side of the fruit on a board and slice down. Cut it as fine or as coarse as you wish. Tie up the pips loosely in a muslin bag. Put the fruit, pips and fruit juices in a very large bowl or two bowls. Leave to soak for 24–48 hours. Cover the bowl to prevent any dust getting in. When the fruit has been soaking for a few hours and I want the peel finer, I cut it up again with scissors while it is still in the bowl. This is reasonably quick.

Put the peel, juices and pips in a large pan and cook gently until the peel is really tender (this may take about 1½ hours). You can test it by taking out a piece of peel and, when it has cooled, pressing it between thumb and finger. It should be quite soft and disintegrate. Remove the bag of pips, squeeze out any liquid. Add the sugar, 1 lb. to each 1 pint of marmalade. (Measure liquid carefully.) Stir until the sugar is dissolved, put the marmalade back on the heat, bring it to the boil and boil vigorously until setting point is reached (see page 26). Remove any scum. Let the marmalade cool slightly until a skin forms. This prevents the peel rising to the top of the jar. Stir gently to distribute the peel evenly. Pour into just-warm jars. Put on the waxed disc at once and cover when cold.

Dark Chunky Marmalade

1½ lb. Seville oranges *3 pints water*
juice of 1 large lemon *3 lb. dark brown sugar*

Wash the fruit thoroughly, cut it in half and squeeze out the juice. Cut the peel into thickish chunks, about ½ in. long. Tie up the pips loosely in a muslin bag. Put the peel, pips, orange and lemon juice in the water, leave for at least 24 hours. Pour it into the pan and simmer gently for 1½–2 hours or until the peel is quite tender. Remove the bag of pips, pressing out the liquid. Add the sugar, let it dissolve, then boil rapidly until setting point is reached. Remove any scum, let the marmalade cool a little. When a skin forms, stir to distribute the peel. Pot and cover.

Family Marmalade

This is a medium marmalade, neither coarse nor fine. It suits most tastes.

- 1 lb. Seville oranges
- ½ lb. sweet oranges
- juice of 1 large lemon
- 2 pints water
- 3 lb. sugar (granulated or preserving)

Wash the fruit thoroughly. Leave it whole and cook it gently with the 2 pints of water in a covered pan for 2 hours. Remove the fruit and when it is cool enough to handle, cut it up into medium-fine strips. Do this on a large plate so as not to lose any of the juice; keep it to be added later. Tie up the pips in a muslin bag. Boil them briskly, in the water the fruit was cooked in, for 10 minutes. This extracts the pectin. Remove the pips, pressing out the juice into the pan. Now add the sliced oranges and their juice, the lemon juice and the sugar. Stir and let the sugar dissolve slowly, then boil quickly until setting point is reached. Remove scum. Let the marmalade cool a little in the pan, stir to distribute the peel. Pot and cover.

When an orange flavour would improve a marinade, 2–3 tablespoons of this marmalade can be used instead of fresh oranges.

Four Fruit Marmalade

- 1 grapefruit
- 2 lemons
- 1 sweet orange
- 1 tangerine

} to make about 1½ lb. fruit

- 3 pints water
- 3 lb. sugar

Wash the fruit, peel it and cut up the peel. Remove any excess pith. Cut up the fruit pulp, remove pips, tie them and any pith in a muslin bag. Put fruit, peel, pips and pith, and water, into a preserving pan. Simmer until peel is quite soft. Remove pips and pith, pressing out the juice into the pan. Add the sugar, let is dissolve, then boil vigorously until setting point is reached. Remove scum. Let the marmalade cool a little in the pan, stir to distribute the peel. Pot and cover.

Grapefruit Marmalade

1½ *lb. grapefruit*
2 *lemons*
3 *pints water*
3 *lb. sugar*

Wash the fruit. Cut in half and squeeze out the juice. If there is a lot of pith on the grapefruit, remove some of it and add it to the pips in a muslin bag. Slice the peel of grapefruits and lemons finely and cut it into ½ in. lengths. Soak the peel, pips and pith in the water and fruit juices overnight. Cook gently for about 2 hours or until the peel has softened. Remove the bag of pips and pith, pressing out the juice into the pan. Add the sugar, let it dissolve, then boil rapidly until setting point is reached. Remove scum. Let the marmalade cool a little in the pan, stir to distribute the fruit. Pot and cover.

Green Tomato Marmalade

3 *lb. green tomatoes*
3 *large, thin-skinned sweet oranges*
juice of 2 *large lemons*
3 *lb. sugar*

Wash the tomatoes and oranges, slice them finely. Tie any of the citrus pips loosely in a muslin bag. Put all the fruit, juice and pips in a bowl, add the sugar and leave for 24 hours. The next day put it all into a pan, bring to the boil and cook gently until the tomatoes are tender and the marmalade is quite thick. Remove the bag of pips, squeeze out the juice into the pan. Pot and cover.

This marmalade can be used as a side dish with curries as it has a sharpish flavour. It can also be used as a breakfast marmalade or to sandwich a sponge cake.

Orange Jelly Marmalade

equal quantity of Seville and sweet oranges
juice of 2 large lemons
3 pints water to each 1 lb. fruit
1 lb. sugar to each 1 pint juice

Wash the fruit, weigh it, squeeze out the juice. Cut up the peel and pulp finely. Tie up the pips in a muslin bag. Cover peel, fruit and pips with the required amount of water. Add the fruit juices. Cook until the peel is tender and looks transparent. Leave to drip overnight in a jelly bag. The next day measure the juice, add the required amount of sugar. Put the sugar and liquid in the pan, let the sugar dissolve, then boil vigorously until setting point is reached. Remove scum. Pot and cover.

Lemon Jelly Marmalade

Lemon jelly marmalade can be made in the same way. Allow $3\frac{1}{4}$ pints of water and 3 lb. of sugar to 2 lb. of lemons.

West Indian Lime Marmalade

1¼ *lb. limes (9–12 according to size)*
2 *lemons*
3 *pints water*
3 *lb. sugar*

Wash the fruit, cut it in half and squeeze out the juice. Slice the peel finely. Tie up the pips in a muslin bag. Add the fruit juices to the water and soak the peel and pips for 24 hours. Pour into a preserving pan, and boil gently until peel is tender. Remove the pips, pressing out the juice into the pan. Add the sugar, let it dissolve slowly, then boil rapidly until setting point is reached. Remove scum. Let the marmalade cool a little in the pan, stir to distribute the peel. Pot and cover.

This marmalade has the unique flavour of limes and is good as a side dish with curries. It can also be spread on toast or used as a filling for a sandwich cake.

Pressure Cooker Marmalade

1½ *lb. Seville oranges*
juice of 1 *large lemon*
1½ *pints water*
3 *lb. sugar*

5 lb. marmalade is normally the maximum amount that a pressure cooker pan will take. Less water is needed in this recipe as there is no evaporation. Remove the rack from the pressure cooker. Wash the fruit, put it whole into the pan. Add the water and lemon juice, put on the lid but keep the vent open. Heat slowly. When steam appears, close the vent and bring the pressure to 15 lb. Cook for 20 minutes. Remove the pan from the heat. Leave for 10 minutes, then remove the

fruit. Cut it up, then put it back in the liquid. Add the sugar and pips tied up in muslin. Let the sugar dissolve, then boil it quickly in the open pan until setting point is reached. Remove bag of pips, press out the juice into the pan. Allow to cool a little, stir. Pot and cover.

SAVOURY RECIPES USING MARMALADE

Glazed Sweet Potatoes

These go extremely well with boiled bacon.

3–4 *sweet potatoes according to size*
4 *oz. orange jelly marmalade (see page* 102)
½ *oz. butter*
2 *tablespoons water*

Wash the potatoes, boil them in salted water until tender. Let them cool, then remove skins. Cut into round slices about ½ in. thick. Put the marmalade, butter and water in a large saucepan (as the potatoes are added later). Stir and cook slowly until the marmalade has melted. Add the potatoes, cook and turn them constantly until they are glazed all over. Take care they do not burn.

Boiled Pork with Orange Sauce

Serves 4–6

2–2½ lb. lean stewing pork (leg, hand or spring)
fat for frying
a veal bone
5–6 young carrots cut in half lengthwise
1 sliced onion
2 oz. sliced mushrooms
bouquet garni (see page 193)
1 tablespoon tomato concentrate
pepper and salt
1 wineglass of dry white wine
water
3 tablespoons Seville orange marmalade (see page 100)
beurre manié (see Glossary, page 223)
chopped parsley

Brown the meat on all sides. Put it in a pan and add the veal bone, carrots, onion, mushrooms, bouquet garni, tomato concentrate, pepper and salt to taste, wine and enough water to cover the ingredients. Put the lid on the pan and simmer gently for 1½–2 hours, depending on the thickness of the meat. When it is cooked, remove and keep hot. Remove bouquet garni and veal bone. Stir the marmalade into the sauce, add small pieces of the beurre manié, stir until the sauce thickens. Cook for 3–4 minutes. Taste for seasoning. Carve the meat, pour the sauce over, sprinkle with chopped parsley. Leaf spinach or a spinach purée goes well with this dish.

Orange Stuffed Pork Rolls

Serves 4-6

1½–2 lb. pork fillet
crushed clove of garlic
pepper
salt
sprinkling of chopped sage leaves
3–4 tablespoons marmalade
flour
butter for frying

Cut the pork into long strips. Flatten them, rub them over with the garlic. Season with freshly ground pepper and salt. Spread with marmalade, sprinkle with chopped sage. Roll up the strips, and secure with a cocktail stick or tie them up. Season with pepper and salt, cover them with a little flour. Fry in hot butter until they are brown all over.

FOR THE GRAVY

2 oz. cooked sliced mushrooms
2 tablespoons marmalade (diluted with 1 tablespoon hot water)
5 fluid oz. sour cream
pepper and salt

Mix together all the ingredients, pour them over the pork rolls, cover the pan and cook gently for 30–40 minutes. Serve with the sauce poured over the rolls.

Wild Duck with Bigarade Sauce

Bigarade is a type of bitter orange; it is used in making Curaçao and it also makes a flavourful sauce to serve with wild duck, duck, pork and venison. I make my sauce with tangy home made coarse-cut marmalade when there are no Seville oranges about.

a brace of wild ducks for 4 people
2 tablespoons bitter orange marmalade (see page 98)
pepper and salt
melted butter
1 large peeled and quartered orange and watercress to garnish

Pepper and salt the birds inside, them put a tablespoon of marmalade in each bird. Brush all over with melted butter.

Cook in a hot oven (425°F) for 20–30 minutes. The birds should not be overcooked. Keep them hot while you make the sauce.

FOR THE SAUCE

1 tablespoon wine vinegar	scant 1 oz. flour
1 oz. sugar	3 tablespoons marmalade (see page 98)
½ pint brown stock	
2 oz. butter	pepper and salt if necessary

Put the sugar and vinegar into the baking tin, stir and scrape the bottom to incorporate any drippings from the ducks, heat slowly until the sugar begins to colour. Add the stock, boil briskly for 5 minutes. Work the butter and flour together (this is called beurre manié), stir small pieces of it into the gravy. Cook until it thickens, add the marmalade, season if necessary. Pour the sauce into a sauceboat. Arrange the ducks on a dish, and decorate with the orange quarters and watercress.

Veal and Orange

Serves 4

¾–1 lb. veal fillet   fat for frying

FOR THE MARINADE

4 large tablespoons orange marmalade (see page 99) or Four Fruit marmalade (see page 100)	3 tablespoons water
	1 tablespoon Worcestershire sauce
	1 teaspoon salt

Heat marmalade and water together, add Worcestershire sauce and salt. Let it get cold.

Cut the veal into thin strips. Marinate for 3–4 hours, turning the meat from time to time. Remove the meat from the marinade, pat it quite dry. Fry it in the fat until brown. Add the marinade, bring to the boil, then simmer for 20–25 minutes. Serve with a purée of potatoes.

SWEET RECIPES USING MARMALADE

Baked Pears with Marmalade Sauce

4–6 pears (according to size), peeled, halved and cored
juice of 1 large lemon

3–4 tablespoons orange jelly marmalade (see page 102)
2 oz. sugar
1 gill hot water

Arrange the pears cut side up in a shallow fireproof dish. Sprinkle them with lemon juice to prevent discoloration. Put some marmalade on each pear and a nob of butter on top. Dissolve the sugar in the hot water, boil for 3–4 minutes. Pour it round the pears. Bake in a moderate oven (350°F) for about 30 minutes, or until the pears are cooked. Cooking time varies considerably with the type of pear. Baste from time to time with the sauce. Serve hot or cold.

Marmalade Tart

Line a pie plate or flan ring with 4 oz. shortcrust pastry (see Appendix, page 220). Half fill it with marmalade. Bake at 425°F for 15–16 minutes. Serve hot or cold.

Marronmarma Cream

8 oz. tin of sweetened chestnut purée or 8 oz. chestnut jam (see page 40)
3 fluid oz. double cream
equal quantity of rich milk

2 tablespoons Family Marmalade (see page 100)
1 tablespoon brandy or Curaçao if liked

If using tinned chestnut purée, beat it well; this makes it lighter and incorporates all the syrup, which usually sinks to the bottom of the tin. Whip the cream and milk together until thick. Mix chestnut and whipped cream together, fold in the marmalade and brandy or Curaçao if you are using either. Spoon into small ramekins or bowls. Chill and serve with a crystallised violet on top.

Vermicelli Pudding

Serves 4-6

3 oz. vermicelli
1 pint milk
2 oz. butter
3 eggs

2 oz. caster sugar
2 tablespoons West Indian marmalade (see page 103)

Heat the milk, add the vermicelli, cook gently for 15 minutes, add the butter. Leave to cool. Lightly butter a fireproof dish, cover the bottom with the marmalade. When the vermicelli is quite cold, add the eggs and butter well beaten together. Put the mixture on top of the marmalade. Bake at 350°F for 1 hour. Serve hot.

Candying

Introduction and Definitions

Candying Tinned Fruit
Candying Fresh Fruit
Using up Surplus Candying Syrup
Candied Angelica Stalks
Marrons Glacés
Candied Orange Peel
Candied Lemon Peel
Candied Grapefruit Peel

SAVOURY RECIPE USING CANDIED FRUIT

Fruity Mustard Sauce

SWEET RECIPES USING CANDIED FRUIT

Bread and Butter Pudding
Chocolate Orange Matchsticks
Creole Punch
Frozen Candied Fruit Custard

CANDYING

INTRODUCTION AND DEFINITIONS

Candied fruits are processed by a slow soaking in strong sugar syrup. They are not at all difficult to do, but time-consuming, because you must spend 15–20 minutes a day for about 2 weeks. At first they are put into a light sugar syrup; its density is increased each day until the syrup is very heavy. The fruit should be impregnated with the syrup and then dried off. Most fruits, the peel of citrus fruits, and angelica stalks, and chestnuts, can all be candied.

Choose fruits with a distinct and characteristic flavour, otherwise their taste may be swamped by the sweetness. Either fresh fruits or tinned fruits can be candied. The process is slightly different because tinned fruit has already absorbed quite a lot of sugar; therefore it can be steeped in a higher sugar concentration to begin with than fresh fruit. If fresh fruit is processed too quickly it shrivels. The water in the fruit must be gradually replaced by the syrup. This is called osmosis (see Glossary, page 225).

Candied fruits are fruits prepared in a plain syrup.

Crystallised fruits are candied fruits covered with granulated sugar. This is the easiest way to crystallise fruit: Dip the candied fruit in boiling water, remove at once, let it drain. Put granulated sugar on greaseproof paper and roll the fruit in it.

Glacé fruits are candied fruits with a shiny finish. Dissolve 1 lb. granulated sugar in ¼ pint of water, bring it to the boil. Pour a little in a basin. Cover the rest of the syrup to prevent evaporation and keep it hot.

Put the candied fruit (or chestnuts) in boiling water, leave for about 20 seconds. Let it drain. Stick the fruit (or chestnuts) on a fine skewer, put it in the syrup, remove it at once, then drain it on a wire grid or tray. Whenever the syrup you are using becomes murky, replace it with the fresh syrup which is being kept hot.

CANDYING

When all the fruit has been glazed, put the grid or tray in a very cool oven – it must not be higher than 120°F or the fruit will lose its shiny look. Gently turn the fruit so that it dries evenly all over. The fruit is ready when it is no longer sticky.

If you are keen on the idea of candying it is worthwhile buying a hydrometer (see Glossary, page 224). This shows the density of the syrup in which the fruit is being processed. But the job can be done quite quickly and efficiently without one.

CANDYING TINNED FRUIT

As tinned fruit is already cooked in the canning process, it takes less time to candy. The first steps have already been taken. The fruit has been prepared and tenderised. Use only the best quality because it is not worthwhile processing fruit of inferior quality. Try tinned pineapple, small whole apricots or firm apricot halves, firm peach halves or slices, whole figs, and guava halves with the seeds removed.

Open the tins of fruit. Drain off the syrup and measure it. You should need about ½ pint of syrup to each 1 lb. of fruit. As the weight on most tins includes solids and liquid you will have to weigh the fruit. First weigh a basin, then drain the fruit, putting it into the basin until the weight is 1 lb. plus the weight of the basin. To each ½ pint of syrup from the fruit add ½ lb. sugar (or sugar and glucose in equal quantities).

If there is less than ½ pint of syrup from the tins of fruit, add enough water to make up to ½ pint. The fruit must always be covered with syrup.

PRESERVING WITH SUGAR

First day Put the fruit in a bowl. Add the sugar to the syrup, bring it slowly to the boil, then pour it over the fruit. Leave for 24 hours.

Second day Pour the syrup off into a saucepan, add 2 oz. sugar (or half sugar, half glucose). Stir to dissolve, slowly bring to the boil, pour it once again over the fruit. Leave for 24 hours.

Third day Repeat (add 2 oz. sugar, dissolve, bring to the boil, cover fruit again with the syrup. Leave for 24 hours).

Fourth day Repeat above procedure.

Fifth day **Note this is different.** Put the syrup into the pan, add 3 *oz*. sugar, heat and stir until dissolved. Add the fruit, bring to the boil. Simmer for 3 minutes. Pour fruit and syrup back into bowl, cover, and leave for 48 hours.

Seventh day Put syrup in the pan, add 3 oz. sugar, heat and stir until dissolved. Add the fruit, bring to the boil. Simmer for 3 minutes. Pour back into the bowl. Cover. Leave for 4 days.

As the syrup cools, it should by this time look rather like thick honey, thick and syrupy. You can test it by putting a little on a saucer to cool. If it is thin, put it back in the pan, add another 3 oz. of sugar, heat and stir until dissolved. Add the fruit, boil for 3 minutes and leave for a further 4 days.

If you want to use the fruit soon, remove it from the syrup, then let it drain on a rack over a large dish or plate. When it has drained thoroughly, put it in a very cool oven (100°F–120°F), and let it dry. It should be turned from time to time as it dries out, to allow the whole fruit to dry. This can take a few hours or 2–3 days. When it is ready it is no longer sticky. It can be dried out in the sun. If you do not want to use the fruit at once, it can be left in the syrup for a few weeks in a cool place, and then dried. The fruit can be given a crystallised or glacé finish (see page 112).

It should be packed in strong cardboard or wooden boxes. Separate the layers with waxed paper. It can also be kept in wide-mouthed jars, but these should not be airtight or the fruit may grow mould. The jars should be covered with paper and tied down.

CANDYING FRESH FRUIT

The fruit should be ripe but still firm and at the peak of perfection. Over-ripe fruit is no good at all; it will disintegrate while being processed. The fruit must be prepared first: Small apricots, greengages and nectarines can be preserved whole or halved. When they are candied whole, they should be pricked gently all over with a silver fork so that the syrup can penetrate.

Cherries should have the stones removed carefully.

Peaches should be peeled and halved.

Pears should be peeled, and cored or not as you like. The stem can be left on.

When the fruit has been prepared, put it in boiling water so that it is just covered, then simmer until it is tender. The time will vary according to the fruit. Over-cooking spoils the taste and texture.

For each 1 lb. of fruit make a syrup with $\frac{1}{2}$ pint of the water the fruit was cooked in and 6 oz. granulated sugar (or sugar and glucose in equal quantities). (You will notice that here there is 2 oz. less sugar than there is to start with in the syrup for candying tinned fruit. This is because the fresh fruit cannot absorb such a high percentage of sugar at this stage.) The fruit must always be covered with the syrup. If there is not enough,

PRESERVING WITH SUGAR

make another batch of the same strength: 6 oz. sugar to ½ pint of water.

First day   Drain the fruit, put it into a bowl. Heat the syrup, stir to dissolve, bring to the boil, pour it over the fruit. Leave for 24 hours.

Second day   Drain off the syrup, add 2 oz. sugar to syrup, bring to the boil, pour it over the fruit. Leave for 24 hours.

Third day   Drain off syrup, add 2 oz. sugar, bring to the boil, pour it over the fruit. Leave for 24 hours.

Fourth day   Drain off syrup, add 2 oz. sugar, bring to the boil, pour it over the fruit. Leave for 24 hours.

Fifth day   Drain off syrup, add 2 oz. sugar, bring to the boil, pour it over the fruit. Leave for 24 hours.

Sixth day   Drain off syrup, add 2 oz. sugar, bring to the boil, pour it over the fruit. Leave for 24 hours.

Seventh day   Drain off syrup, add 2 oz. sugar, bring to the boil, pour it over the fruit, Leave for 24 hours.

12 oz. of sugar has now been added to the first syrup.

Eighth day   **Note this is different.** Drain off syrup, add 3 oz. sugar, heat and stir until dissolved. Add the fruit, bring to the boil. Simmer for 3 minutes. Pour back into bowl. Leave for 48 hours.

Tenth day   Drain off syrup, add 3 oz. sugar, heat and stir until dissolved. Add the fruit, bring to the boil. Simmer for 3 minutes. Pour back into bowl. Leave for 4 days.

The syrup should be really thick (see page 114).

Dry out fruit in a cool oven or in the sun (see page 114).

Finish it off by giving it a crystallised or glacé finish (see page 112).

To store, see page 115.

CANDYING

USING UP SURPLUS CANDYING SYRUP

Do not throw away any left-over syrup. It can be kept for some time, as the high sugar content preserves it. In France bottles of sugar syrup are on sale for use in the kitchen whenever a syrup is required. It is not usually obtainable in this country except for the manufacturing trade.

It can be used for sweetening stewed fruit, fruit salads, sauces; added to drinks, such as Creole Punch (see page 122); and used in liqueurs of the same flavour (i.e. a syrup that has been used to candy orange peel, for an orange-flavoured liqueur).

Candied Angelica Stalks

If you can get fresh angelica, do candy some. Only use the young stalks, which are best picked in late April and May. Strip off the leaves, two or three can be added to a salad to give a pleasant, aromatic, unusual flavour. Put the stalks in boiling water and cook them for about 10 minutes or until they have softened. Drain them and with a sharp knife scrape off the outside, fibrous layer. Cut the stalks into 3–4 in. lengths. Put them in a bowl. Make a syrup with 1 lb. sugar (or half sugar and glucose) and 1 pint of water. Stir until it is dissolved, then bring to the boil. If the colour is as important to you as the flavour, the bright green of the commercial angelica can be obtained by adding a few drops of green vegetable colouring to the syrup. Pour the syrup over the stalks. Cover and leave for 24 hours.

Now follow the directions for Candying Fresh Fruit (see page 115) starting from the second day. When the stalks are processed they can be left in the syrup for a few weeks and then dried out, or dried out straight away (see page 114). When they are dry put them into jars and store them in a dark cupboard.

TO USE ANGELICA

Cut the stalks into attractive shapes to decorate cakes, trifles and other sweets. Chopped angelica can be added to cakes and puddings.

Marrons Glacés

As it is difficult to keep the chestnuts whole while they are being processed, buy at least 2 lb. There are sure to be some casualties, but they need not be wasted; the flavour is just as good.

2 lb. Italian or Spanish chestnuts   *½ lb. glucose*
1½ lb. granulated sugar   *3 gills water*

Make a gash in the chestnuts with a sharp knife. Put a few at a time into boiling water, leave for about 3 minutes. Remove from the water, add some more, and continue in this way until all the chestnuts have been left in boiling water. When you can handle them, remove the outer and inner skins. When they are all peeled, put them in a bowl of cold water.

Make the syrup. Put sugar, glucose and water in a heavy pan. It must be large enough to take all the chestnuts. Bring to the boil, drain the chestnuts, add them. Bring up to boiling point. Turn off the heat. Cover and leave until the next day in a warm place if possible. Bring chestnuts and syrup slowly to the boil, turn off heat, leave again until the next day. The third and last day, (as the nuts are not juicy like fruit they only need to be processed for 3 days), bring chestnuts and syrup again to the boil. Remove chestnuts and any pieces, drain them on a rack.

To give a glacé finish see page 112. Wrap the whole chestnuts carefully in foil. Pack in the same way as candied fruit (see page 115). The small pieces can be eaten at once.

Candied Orange Peel

Choose, large, thick-skinned oranges. Wash the fruit well. Remove the peel with a sharp knife: make an incision right round the orange, from the stalk end downwards, and back to stalk end; then do this the other way, so that the orange peel is quartered. Carefully remove it. Put the peel in a pan with enough boiling water to cover it, let it boil gently for 1 hour. Drain, boil a second time in fresh water until the peel has softened, add more water if required. Drain the peel. Make a syrup with 2 oz. sugar to each 1 gill of water. Put it in a pan, stir until dissolved, bring to the boil. Put the orange peel in a basin, cover with the syrup, leave for 24 hours.

Now follow the instructions for candied fresh fruit.

Candied Lemon Peel

This is done in the same way as orange peel.

Candied Grapefruit Peel

This is done in the same way as orange peel, but the water should be changed 3 or 4 times when the peel is being cooked in the first place.

SAVOURY RECIPE USING CANDIED FRUIT

Fruity Mustard Sauce

This is a good sauce to serve with roast guinea-fowl or with boiled or baked ham.

½ *pint white sauce*
1–2 *teaspoons dry mustard*
1 *teaspoon spiced vinegar (see page 153)*

sugar to taste
1–2 *tablespoons chopped candied fruit (see pages 113–6)*
½ *oz. butter*

FOR THE WHITE SAUCE

¾ *oz. butter*
¾ *oz. flour*

½ *pint hot milk*
pepper and salt to taste

Melt the butter, add the flour, stir and cook for 3 minutes. Remove from the heat and add the liquid, beating vigorously. Put the sauce back on the heat, bring to boiling point, cook and beat for 3 minutes. Add pepper and salt.

Dilute the mustard with the vinegar and add it to the sauce, with sugar, candied fruit and the butter. Stir to mix well. Serve hot.

SWEET RECIPES USING CANDIED FRUIT

Bread and Butter Pudding

thin slices of white bread and butter (crusts removed)
1 pint milk
grated rind of 1 lemon
6 blanched and chopped almonds
2½ oz. caster sugar
1 gill double cream
5 eggs
1 small wine glass of brandy or sherry
1½ oz. chopped candied peel (see page 119)
3 oz. sultanas
grated nutmeg

Scald the milk, together with the grated lemon rind and almonds. Add the sugar, stir until it is dissolved. Let it cool, then gradually add the cream. Beat the eggs until they are light and frothy, add the milk and cream to them, stirring all the time, then add sherry or brandy. Well butter a fireproof dish, line it with the bread and butter. Sprinkle sultanas, candied peel and nutmeg on top of the bread. Add a layer of bread and butter on top of that. Continue until the dish is ¾ full. Pour the egg and milk mixture slowly over the bread and fruit. Leave it for 2 hours so that the bread becomes impregnated. Bake in a moderate oven (350°F) for 45–60 minutes. The top should be brown.

Chocolate Orange Matchsticks

matchstick strips of candied orange peel (see page 119)
plain chocolate for coating

PRESERVING WITH SUGAR

Break up the chocolate. Put it in a bowl over a pan of boiling water. Turn off the heat. Stir until the chocolate melts. Put in the orange strips. Remove them carefully. Put them on a piece of lightly oiled greaseproof paper. Leave until the chocolate has set. Any left-over chocolate may be used again.

Creole Punch

A way to use up left-over candying syrup.

Put $\frac{1}{5}$ syrup to $\frac{4}{5}$ rum and a zest of lemon in a glass. Mix thoroughly until the syrup is completely incorporated. Add plenty of ice cubes.

If you want to make enough punch for several people, put the sugar syrup, rum and lemon peel in a shaker, adding plenty of crushed ice. Shake very well before serving.

Frozen Candied Fruit Custard

$1\frac{1}{2}$ *pints custard (see page* 66)
vanilla essence to taste
3 *tablespoons brandy or sherry*

8 *oz. finely chopped mixed candied fruit (cherries, peaches, pineapple, see pages* 113–6)

Soak the candied fruit in the alcohol. Make the custard; flavour it with vanilla essence. Set refrigerator to maximum cold. Put the custard in the freezing trays in the freezing compartment; do not put the fruit in at this stage. Stir from time to time as the custard freezes. When it is stiff, remove from the trays, put it in an ice cold bowl and mix in the soaked fruit with the alcohol. Re-freeze, stirring 2 or 3 times while the mixture is freezing. Serve in glasses, with whipped cream on top and a jam sauce poured over (see page 62).

Preserving by Sterilisation and Vacuum

Introduction

Fruit Bottling
Bottling and Using Bottled Fruit

Fruit Syrups and Juices
Making and Using Fruit Syrups and Juices

INTRODUCTION

When fruit is plentiful, either on your own trees or in the market, you can preserve it and spread its flavour throughout the year, even without the luxury of a deep freeze. Bottled fruit can be used in the same way as cooked fresh fruit, for pies, tarts, fruit salads and puddings. In fact for any cooked fruit recipe.

Fruit can be preserved by sterilisation and vacuum in a number of ways – slow, quick, in the oven, on top of the cooker in a pan of water, or in a pressure cooker. The method I prefer is the quick water pan way, because it is easy and virtually foolproof, if you follow the simple rules.

EQUIPMENT

Little, if any, special equipment is needed, except specially designed screw band or clip top jars and a saucepan with a perforated false bottom with handles for easy removing from the pan.

Fruit Bottling Pan If you do not want the expense of buying a special pan you can improvise with an old-fashioned fish kettle or a deep saucepan. You can make a false bottom for the saucepan with wooden slats, thick towelling or cardboard so that the jars are kept off the bottom of the pan. Always put a folded cloth or newspaper between the jars to prevent them touching each other and also to keep them from the sides of the pan. The pan *must* be deep enough for the jars to be completely covered with water. This is essential. The fruit must be completely sterilised by heat to destroy the moulds and yeasts which are present on all fruit, and also to stop further growth of bacteria and to arrest the activity of enzymes.

Jars Jars must be scrupulously clean and free from cracks or chips. They may be used over and over again. Screw bands and clips should be washed, dried thoroughly and the metal parts brushed lightly with olive oil to prevent oxydisation. Keep them wrapped up for the next batch of fruit bottling. Rubber rings should be perfect.

Screw Top Jars These can have glass or metal tops with rubber rings which create a seal, and metal screw bands. They must always be scrupulously clean. After screwing the filled jars down tightly, give them a $\frac{1}{4}$ turn in reverse so that steam and air can escape while the fruit is being processed. When the jars are removed from the pan, immediately after processing, they must be screwed as tightly as possible to create a vacuum. The screw bands may have to be tightened once or twice during the cooling time. The lacquer coating inside metal lids should be unscratched.

Clip Jars These have a spring clip and are really designed for safety, as the steam escapes automatically during sterilisation. When cooling, the clip holds the lid tightly in position so that a vacuum is formed. Take care not to scratch metal lids when fitting clips.

Heatproof glove A heatproof glove or a thick cloth is necessary if you do not want to burn your hands when handling hot jars.

Knives Use a silver or stainless steel knife when peeling fruit.

Potato peeler A stainless steel one is useful for paring fruit thinly.

INTRODUCTION

Cherry pitter For easy removal of cherry stones.
Thermometer This is optional *except* for the cold water pan method.

BOTTLING FLUIDS

Fruit can be bottled in water or in a sugar syrup. Sugar syrup brings out the flavour of the fruit and keeps it a better colour. As syrup is more buoyant than water the fruit is inclined to float to the top; this does not affect the flavour or the goodness. Pack the fruit tightly but leave enough room for the water or syrup.

Sugar syrup 8 oz. of granulated or loaf sugar to 1 pint of water is a good standard syrup. For very sour fruit use 10–11 oz. sugar to 1 pint of water. You can use more or less sugar according to personal taste and the sweetness of the fruit, but do not go below 5 oz. sugar to the pint. You can always add more sugar when the fruit is to be eaten, but there is little to be done if the syrup is too sweet. Dissolve the sugar in the water, bring to the boil and boil for 1–2 minutes.

THINGS TO LOOK OUT FOR

Mould and Fermentation When this occurs it is unsafe to use the fruit and it should be thrown away. Mould can be caused by:
  Insufficient time allowed for sterilisation.
  Temperatures too low.

If jars are not completely submerged in the water when being processed.

If vacuum is broken.

When fruit is over-ripe fermentation is more likely but it does not occur unless the hermetic seal is broken.

Broken Vacuum Seal When air enters a jar the fruit deteriorates in various ways. It may form moulds or fermentation, or harmful bacteria may get in. A minute hole in a rubber ring can prevent a perfect vacuum. Always examine them thoroughly for holes, or to see if they have perished. It is safer to use rings only once. Soak them in warm water for 15 minutes, then dip them in boiling water before putting them on the jars.

Sometimes a piece of fruit or syrup prevents the lid forming a complete vacuum. The lid may be held in position while it is being tested, but at a later date as the syrup dries off a leak may develop.

Deposit Minerals in hard water may be precipitated to form a crystalline deposit or sediment at the bottom of the jar. (See note on soft water, page 23). This is harmless.

Fruit Discoloration If jars filled with fruit are not completely submerged in water when they are being processed, the fruit at the top of the jars will be insufficiently cooked and will discolour.

Fruit such as apples and pears should be put in acidulated water immediately they are prepared (before they are put into the jars), to prevent oxydisation (see page 225). If plums and pears are processed at too low a temperature they may discolour.

Fruit rising to the top of the jar This does not affect either the flavour or the goodness of the fruit. It is invariably caused by the sugar syrup. Pack the fruit tightly without bruising it.

Fruit Bottling

Preparation and Processing of Different Fruit Groups:
  Berries
  Drupes
  Pomes

RECIPES USING BOTTLED FRUIT

Cherry and Almond Tart   German Obstorte (see page 92)

PREPARATION AND PROCESSING OF DIFFERENT FRUIT GROUPS

QUICK WATER PAN METHOD

Remember that different fruits need different processing times. What you want to preserve is fruit, not syrup, and so you should pack as much fruit in the jars as possible without bruising or spoiling the shape. The more fruit there is in the jar, the longer it takes to process. For example, loosely packed raspberries will take 2 minutes, tightly packed they will take 10 minutes.

The 3 main groups most suitable for bottling are:

1. BERRIES

Bilberries, blackberries; cranberries (when available fresh); black, white and red currants; gooseberries, loganberries, mulberries, raspberries, strawberries, whortleberries.

Preparation Pick over the fruit; remove any leaves, calyxes and stems. Wash if dirty. Top and tail gooseberries and prick each one to prevent them shrivelling when they are processed.

To Process Berries Prepare the fruit, pack it into warm jars, fill to the brim with hot sugar syrup (140°F if you are using a sugar thermometer, see page 27). Dip the rubber rings in boiling water, put them on the jars, then put on the lids and the screw bands or clips. When using screw bands, screw them up tightly then give a ¼ turn in reverse. Put the jars carefully in the prepared pan, cover them completely with warm water (about 100°F – just above blood heat). Cover the pan with the lid, bring water to simmering point (190°F). This should take from 25–30 minutes. Keep at this temperature for 10 minutes. Remove jars from pan one at a time, tighten screw bands. Cool. Tighten screw bands as the fruit is cooling if necessary. The next day unscrew the bands or remove clips. Lift each jar up by the lid. If the seal is perfect, it will stay firmly attached to the jar. If not, the lid will come away in your hand and the fruit must be processed again or used right away.

Label and store in a dark, cool place.

2. DRUPES

Apricots, cherries, damsons, greengages, nectarines, peaches, plums.

Preparation Always choose firm, ripe fruit. Wash it, remove stalks and stones if preferred. Apricots can be packed whole or split in half. Wash cherries, pack whole or stone them. When bottling peaches, choose a freestone variety such as Hales. They are pleasanter to eat when skinned. Dip them in boiling water for about 1 minute, then in cold water. The skins should come off quite easily. Pack fruit whole or cut in half or sliced.

To Process Drupes Prepare the fruit, pack it into warm jars, fill to the brim with hot sugar syrup, (140°F if you are using a sugar thermometer, see page 27). Dip the rubber rings in boiling water, put them on the jars, then put on the lids and the screw bands or clips. When using screw bands, screw them up tightly then give a ¼ turn in reverse. Put the jars carefully in the prepared pan, cover them completely with warm water (about 100°F – just above blood heat). Cover the pan with the lid, bring water to simmering point (190°F). This should take from 25–30 minutes. Keep at this temperature for 10 minutes for whole apricots, cherries, greengages and plums. Allow 20 minutes for halved fruit (apricots, peaches, nectarines) because they pack tightly together. Finish off in the same way as berries (see above).

3. POMES

Apples, pears, quinces.

Preparation

Apples   Peel, core and cut into slices or rings. Put them in acidulated water to prevent discoloration (2 tablespoons lemon juice to 1 pint of cold water).

Pears   Only use the best dessert pears. Conference, Doyenne de Comice, and William pears, if you can catch them on their day of perfection, are all excellent. They should be peeled, halved and cored. Put them at once into acidulated water to prevent discoloration.

Quinces   Peel, core and slice them. Put them in acidulated water to prevent discoloration. Only use small jars, as quinces are not often eaten on their own but added to apples, or used as a garnish (see page 88).

To Process Pomes   Proceed in exactly the same way as explained for berries and drupes, but maintain temperature of 190°F (simmering point) for 20 minutes for apples and quinces and 40 minutes for pears.

SUB-TROPICAL AND TROPICAL FRUIT

Although tropical and sub-tropical fruit such as bananas, melons, paw paw, figs and lychees are available here, they are usually too expensive to justify bottling.

Cold Water Pan Method

A thermometer is essential for this method. Pack the fruit into *cold* jars, cover with *cold* water or *cold* syrup. Dip the rubber rings in boiling water, put them on the jars, put the lids on, add screw bands or clips. Give the screw bands a ¼ turn in reverse. Put the jars in the prepared pan (see Quick Water Pan Method, page 129). Cover them completely with *cold* water. Put the lid on the pan, bring the water slowly up to 130°F (this should take about 1½ hours). Then raise the temperature of the water to 165°F for berries and apples. Process the fruit for 10 minutes, i.e. maintain the temperature of 165°F for 10 minutes. Drupes need a temperature of 180°F and the fruit should be processed for 15 minutes. For pears the temperature should be raised to 190°F and the fruit processed for 40 minutes.

Dry Slow Oven Method

I find this method less satisfactory because if oven temperatures are unreliable or erratic, the fruit may be over-cooked and charred. Fill the jars with the fruit, put on the lids, but not the rubber rings or the screw bands or clips. Water or syrup is not added at this stage. Put the jars on a piece of cardboard in the oven at 250°F. Do not put the jars close together but leave room for the air to circulate. Processing time will depend on how many jars are in the oven – the more jars, the longer it will take. Berries will take about 50 minutes for up to 4 lb., and about 70 minutes for 5–10 lb. When fruit is processed, remove the jars, one at a time, and fill up with *boiling* syrup or water. Dip rubber rings in boiling water, put them on the jar, then screw on the bands or fasten the clips. Leave to cool. Test the next day to see if the seal is perfect (see page 130). Label and store.

Wet Moderate Oven Method

This is like the slow oven way, but warm jars are packed with fruit and filled to within an inch of the rim with *boiling* water or syrup. The rubber rings are dipped in boiling water then put on and the lids on top. Screw bands or clips are not fixed in position until later. Arrange a baking tray with layers of newspaper on top, then should the syrup bubble over it will not make such a mess. Do not put the jars close together; the air must circulate. The oven should be pre-heated to 300°F. Berries should be processed for 35 minutes for up to 4 lb., and 50 minutes for 5–10 lb. Remove the jars one at a time, put on the screw bands or clips. Leave to cool. Test the seal (see page 130). Label and store.

Pressure Cooker Method

You can only bottle with your pressure cooker if it is deep enough to take the jars and has a guage which will allow a 5-lb. steam pressure to be maintained without failing. There should be at least 1 in. water in the pan before the rack and bottles are put in.

Pack the fruit in warm jars, add boiling syrup or water to within an inch of the rim. Dip the rings in boiling water and fit on the lids and the clips or screw bands. Screw bands should be given a ¼ turn in reverse. Put the jars on the rack in the pan, put on the lid. Keep the vent open until you see a jet of steam, then close it and bring the pressure up to 5 lb. (this should take from 5–10 minutes). Maintain pressure for 1 minute for berries, cherries, apples, and greengages. For halved apricots, nectarines and peaches maintain pressure for 3–4 minutes. For pears and whole tomatoes maintain pressure for 5 minutes. When fruit is processed, turn off the heat. Leave for 10 minutes before opening the pressure cooker. Remove the jars, tighten screw bands, leave on sheets of cardboard or newspaper to cool. Test for seal the next day (see page 130). Label and store.

RECIPES USING BOTTLED FRUIT

Bottled fruit is used in many recipes for fruit tarts. Here is an unusual one.

Cherry and Almond Tart

6 oz. shortcrust pastry (see Appendix, page 220)

1 jar of bottled cherries
2 tablespoons redcurrant jelly

FOR THE TOPPING

2 oz. butter
2 oz. caster sugar
2 eggs

2 teaspoons flour
2 oz. ground almonds
a few drops of almond essence

Roll out the pastry thinly, line a 7–8 in. sandwich tin. Drain the cherries, remove stones if necessary. Cover the bottom of the pastry with the jelly. Arrange the cherries on top. Now make the topping. Cream butter and sugar together, add the eggs alternately with the flour (to prevent curdling), beat them in thoroughly. Add the ground almonds and almond essence.

Spread it carefully on top of the cherries. Bake at 375°F for 15 minutes, reduce heat to 350°F and cook for 30 minutes. This can be eaten hot or cold.

See also **German Obstorte** (Fruit Salad Tart), page 92.

Fruit Syrups and Juices

Introduction
Pointers to Success

RECIPES

Prototype Recipe: Cherry Syrup
Elderberry Syrup
Ginger Syrup
Lemon Syrup
Orange Syrup
Raspberry or Strawberry Syrup

Rose Hip Syrup
Pomegranate Syrup (Grenadine)
Tomato Juice

Berliner Weisse

FRUIT SYRUPS AND JUICES

INTRODUCTION

Making fruits into syrups and juices is a good way of preserving their flavour. Syrups can be used in many ways; for drinks they can be diluted with water or soda water, or with milk for milk shakes. They can be used in jellies and fruit salads and added to sauces.

PRESERVING BY STERILISATION AND VACUUM

Choose fresh-picked, ripe fruit when the flavour is at its peak. Berries make the best syrups and juices, as the nodules are packed with juice which is easily extracted. Wild blackberries are excellent; they are more distinctive than cultivated ones. Raspberries and strawberries are delicious, although conventional. Raspberry or strawberry syrup is added to Berliner Weisse (see page 146). Loganberries, mulberries, bilberries and elderberries are exceptional.

Fruit Syrups

The simplest way of making fruit syrups at home is by extracting the juice with heat, adding sugar, sterilising and finally hermetically sealing. The minimum of water should be used to keep the full fruit flavour, but the amount depends on the juiciness of the fruit. The amount of sugar too will vary according to the sweetness of the fruit (usually from 8–12 oz. for each 1 pint of juice). The juice can, if liked, be bottled without sweetening and the sugar added when it is used, but the flavour is not so fine. (Juice can also be extracted with a liquidiser or juice separator).

Put the fruit in a double saucepan, or in a bowl that will fit over a saucepan of boiling water. It is this slow cooking which preserves the flavour. As the fruit is heated, press it with a wooden spoon to help the juice escape. When all the juice has been extracted, strain it through a jelly bag overnight. You can squeeze it, because it does not matter if the juice is not perfectly clear.

Add the sugar to the cold juice, stir until it is dissolved, do not heat it. Strain it through a muslin or a fine nylon sieve. Bottle at once in scrupulously clean bottles. Ones with screw stoppers are less trouble, as the corks do not have to be wired down to prevent them popping out as they are heated. Corks and stoppers should be boiled for 15 minutes to sterilise them; they must be under the water all the time.

Fill the bottles to within 1 in. of the top of screw-on covers and 1½ in. if using corks. Screw up tightly, or tie down corks.

Now process the syrup. Arrange the bottles in a deep pan with a false bottom, or put them on a rack or a thick layer of paper. Leave space between the bottles so that the water can circulate. Folds of newspaper can be put between them to keep them upright. Fill the pan with water to come right up to the top of the bottles, but not to cover them. Bring the water to simmering point and keep it simmering for 20 minutes.

Remove bottles, tighten the screw caps, push in the corks as soon as possible. When the syrup is cold, cover the tops of the bottles with a layer of paraffin wax to make a completely airtight seal. The wax should cover the top of the cap or cork and come down the neck of the bottle for about ½ in., rather like the covering over the corks in wine bottles.

Fruit Juices

The same types of fruit are suitable for making fruit juices as for fruit syrups. They can be made in a similar way, but as they are usually drunk undiluted, less sugar is added (about 3 oz. to each 1 pint of juice, varying according to the fruit and its sweetness). Once a bottle is opened it should be kept in a cool place and drunk within 2–3 days.

POINTERS TO SUCCESS

◇ Use ripe fruit at peak of perfection.

◇ Sugar must be completely dissolved before bottling.

◇ When filling the scrupulously clean bottles do not fill right up but leave a space, as syrup and juice expand when heated during processing.

◇ Corks and stoppers should be boiled for at least 15 minutes before being used. Ordinary corks must be wired or tied down before processing; if not, they may blow out. Screw tops are better.

Prototype Recipe: Cherry Syrup

cherries   *8–12 oz. sugar to 1 pint juice*
a little water

Choose juicy cherries, wash them and remove the stems. Do not bother about the stones, but crack some of them so that the flavour from the kernels penetrates the juice. Put the cherries in a basin, press with a wooden spoon to extract the juice, then moisten with a little water and heat very gently until the juice runs. Press from time to time. When it looks as if all the juice has been extracted, strain the juice through a jelly bag overnight. Add sugar to taste (8–12 oz. per 1 pint of juice) to the cold juice, stir until it is dissolved. Strain again through a fine sieve to remove any fruit pulp or fibres. Pour the syrup into bottles; those with screw tops are best. Leave

FRUIT SYRUPS AND JUICES

1 in. at the top for expansion during sterilisation. If you use bottles with corks, the bottles should be filled to within 1½ in. of the top and the corks fastened securely with string or wire to prevent them being forced out by the expansion of the syrup during sterilisation. Corks and stoppers must be sterilised (see page 140). Arrange the bottles in a pan with a false bottom. Leave space between them so that the water can circulate. Folds of newspaper can be put between them to keep them upright. Fill the pan with warm water up to the level of the bottom of the corks. Bring the water to simmering point and simmer for 20 minutes. Remove bottles, tighten screw caps or push in corks as soon as possible. When the syrup is quite cool, and the corks (if used) are dry, dip them in melted paraffin wax so that about ½ in. of the bottle neck is covered (see page 29). This creates a hermetic seal.

Elderberry Syrup

elderberries   12 *oz. sugar to* 1 *pint juice*

You will need plenty of elderberries to get a pint of juice. Stalk them and wash them well. Put them in a heavy pan over a low heat. Press them with a wooden spoon while they are cooking, to help all the juice to run. Strain overnight in a jelly bag. Measure the juice and add the required amount of sugar, stir until it is dissolved, bring to boiling point, cook for 5 minutes. Skim, bottle and process.

If liked spices may be added when the berries are first heated. Cloves, cinnamon and root ginger go well.

For a feverish cold put 1 tablespoon of the syrup in a glass, fill up with boiling water, stir to mix. Grate a little nutmeg on top. It is a very refreshing drink.

Ginger Syrup
(a recipe from Ceylon)

½ *lb. green root ginger (obtainable at Oriental shops)*
2 *lb. sugar*
1 *in. piece of cinnamon*
1 *pint cold water*

Soak the ginger overnight in cold water. Scrape the skin off, and slice the ginger finely. Put ginger, sugar and 1 pint of fresh cold water into a pan, heat and stir until the sugar is dissolved. Cook gently with the lid on until the ginger has softened and the syrup is thick. Remove from heat. Strain through a very fine sieve or muslin. Leave to cool, then bottle.

This syrup can be used in many ways. For a stimulating drink add 1 dessertspoon of ginger syrup and the juice of 1 orange to ½ pint of iced water or soda water.

It can be added to fruit salads, poured over ice cream and used as a sauce for steamed puddings.

Lemon Syrup

12–14 *lemons (or 1 pint lemon juice)*
2½ *lb. sugar (more or less, according to taste*
1½ *pints water*

Wash the fruit. Cut in half and squeeze out the juice with a lemon squeezer. A few strips of peel added when the sugar and water are cooked together gives a more pronounced flavour.

Put peel, sugar and water in a heavy pan, heat and stir until sugar is thoroughly dissolved. Strain. Add the lemon juice,

FRUIT SYRUPS AND JUICES

stir well. Bottle and process (see page 138-9). Colour and flavour deteriorate if syrup is kept for longer than a few weeks.

To make a refreshing drink add about 5 times the amount of water as juice.

Orange Syrup

8-10 large, thin-skinned oranges   *1½ pints water*
  (*or 1 pint orange juice*)   *1 oz. citric acid*
2 lb. sugar (or to taste)

The citric acid adds quite a lot of flavour to the orange syrup. The acid and sugar should always be added to the unheated juice. Wash the oranges thoroughly. Add a few strips of peel to the sugar and water. Heat and stir until the sugar is quite dissolved. Strain. Mix the orange juice with the citric acid and add the sugar and water. Mix well. Bottle and process (see page 138-9).

For an orange drink add water to taste to the orange syrup.

Raspberry or Strawberry Syrup

equal quantities of fruit and sugar

Hull and pick over the fruit, put it in a basin, cover with an equal quantity of sugar. Leave it overnight. The next day mash the berries and rub them through a nylon sieve, or liquidise and strain them. Simmer the juice on a very low heat for 10-15 minutes. Bottle, cork and process (see page 138-9).

This can be added to fruit salads, poured over ice cream and added to fruit cups. See Berliner Weisse (page 146).

Rose Hip Syrup

well-coloured rose hips   *½ lb. sugar to each ¾ pint juice*
water

Wash the rose hips thoroughly, mince them coarsely or put them through a liquidiser with 1 gill of water. Put them in an aluminium or unchipped enamel pan. Bring to the boil and simmer for 30 minutes. Pour the contents of the pan into a bowl, cover and leave overnight. The next morning strain and measure the juice. Add the required amount of sugar, stir to dissolve, boil for 5 minutes. Put the syrup while it is still hot into small bottles; they should be warm too. Process in a pan of hot water for 5 minutes (see page 139). When the bottles are cool, cover the stoppers with paraffin wax (see page 29).

Once the syrup is opened, it does not keep much longer than a week. It should be kept in a cool place. It is a wonderful source of vitamin C; 1 dessertspoonful taken once a day is a good tonic. It can be poured over natural yoghourts and added to soft drinks.

Pomegranate Syrup
(Grenadine)

This syrup is very popular in France and the children love it, diluted with water or lemonade. This is the French method:

pomegranates (abour 12 will give 1 quart of juice)   *1½ lb. sugar to each 1 quart of juice*

Cut the pomegranates in half and squeeze them like lemons with a large lemon squeezer. Alternatively, cut them in half and with a teaspoon carefully scoop out the juicy red seeds, remove any pith. Put the seeds in a bowl and crush them with a wooden spoon. Strain them through a jelly bag, squeeze to get all the juice; or the seeds can be liquidised and strained. The juice, however it is extracted, should be put through a jelly bag. Measure the juice and to each quart allow 1½ lb. sugar. Put it in a pan, heat slowly, stirring until the sugar is dissolved. Boil gently for 10 minutes. Skim if necessary. Pour into warm bottles and cork down. If you want to keep it any length of time when it is bottled, process it (see page 139).

Tomato Juice

tomatoes
to each quart of purée allow:
  ½ pint water
  1 teaspoon salt
  pepper to taste
  1 oz. sugar

Wash the tomatoes, remove the stalks. Cut them up roughly. Put them in a heavy pan and simmer gently, pressing them down with a wooden spoon. When they are quite soft, liquidise and strain them; alternatively, rub them through a fine nylon sieve. Measure the purée and to each 1 quart allow ½ pint of water, 1 teaspoon sea salt, pepper and 1 oz. sugar. Heat and stir, and bring to boiling point. Pour carefully into hot bottles and process (see page 139). Tomato juice can be served chilled, with the usual dash of Worcestershire sauce, or celery salt. It can also be added to savoury dishes instead of stock.

Berliner Weisse

This is a delicious and refreshing drink and a good way of using home made fruit syrups.

1 gill raspberry or strawberry syrup   *½ pint ice-cold light lager*

Pour the fruit juice into a wide-mouthed goblet. In Berlin they have specially large glasses. Add the lager; leave enough room for the froth. Swizzle to mix and serve with 2 drinking straws laid across the top.

Preserving With Vinegar And Spices

Flavoured Vinegars, Chutneys and Pickles
Making and Using Vinegars, Chutneys and Pickles

Flavoured Vinegars, Chutneys And Pickles

VINEGARS

Vinegar Making

Chilli Vinegar
Garlic Vinegar
Shallot Vinegar
Spiced Vinegar

Tarragon Vinegar
Rose Vinegar
Raspberry Vinegar

CHUTNEYS

Introduction
General Hints for Chutney Making (and Pickles)
Pointers to Success

Old Homestead Apple Chutney
Banana and Apple Chutney
Chinese Sweet-Sour Mixed Fruit Chutney
Mixed Fruit Chutney
Gooseberry Chutney

Preserved Stem Ginger Chutney
Lime Chutney
Lemon Chutney
Green Mango Chutney
Siamese Peach Chutney
Pear and Lemon Chutney
Plum Chutney

PICKLES

Best Months for Pickling Vegetables

Pickled Beetroot
Pickled Red Cabbage
Cherries in Spiced Vinegar
Pickled Indian Corn
Pickled Damsons
Pickled Dates
Sweet and Sour Pickled Gherkins
Lime Pickle
Lemon Pickle
Mint Sauce
Clear Mixed Pickle
Pickled Nasturtium Seeds
Piccalilli
Pickled Onions
Pimientos Preserved in Vinegar
Pineapple Pickle
Rhubarb Pickle
Tomato Ketchup
Pickled Walnuts with Sweet Spiced Vinegar
Water Melon Pickle

SAVOURY RECIPES USING CHUTNEY AND PICKLES

Beef Smoore with Peach Chutney
Boeuf Gros Sel
Cheese and Chutney Quiche
Cheese and Chutney Spread
Chicken Siamese Style with Coconut Cream and Sweet-Sour Chutney
Baked Chutney Cheese Rolls
Connoisseur's Carp
Crab and Pickle Canapés
Roast Stuffed Duck with Sweet-Sour Chutney
Eggs in Baked Potatoes with Chutney
Fish Cakes with Lemon Pickle
Ham-Stuffed Marrow
Piquant Stuffed Lamb Shoulder
Baked Meat Loaf
Pickleburgers
Walnut Sauce
Welsh Rarebit with Pickles

SWEET RECIPES

Boiled Batter Pudding with Raspberry Vinegar

Spicy Watermelon Slices

VINEGARS

VINEGAR MAKING

Vinegar is a deviation from the straight and narrow path which produces alcoholic drinks. We have all had half bottles of wine which go round the bend if left in contact with the air too long. It becomes sour, turns into vinegar, and a skin forms. This is known as 'Vinegar Mother'. A fungus, myocerma aceti (acetic acid bacteria), a living organism, causes a second fermentation which produces vinegar.

Once you have your vinegar mother you have to go on feeding it with wine or other suitable fluids such as cider. In return you will get a continuous supply of vinegar for all your needs.

It should be kept in a large jar; one with a wooden tap is the best, and it must *not* be airtight – it is the micro-organisms in the air which do the job. The vinegar mother must be kept supplied with any ends of bottles or dregs of wine or cider. If you are not a wine drinker, add half a bottle of cheap wine from time to time. You can also keep your friends in vinegar, if you give them a piece of the thick, sticky skin which is on top of the liquid and is the 'mother'. It is this layer which does the work. Either red or white wine can be put into the same brew. It should be kept in a fairly warm place (about 60°F–85°F is ideal) so that the bacteria develop. Never touch the vinegar mother with a metal spoon, for this can mean death to her.

Only the best quality vinegar should be used for chutneys, pickles and relishes. If you want a chutney with a delicate flavour such as Pear and Lemon Chutney (page 162) or Chinese Sweet-Sour Mixed Fruit Chutney (page 158), use wine vinegar; these are just two examples. Cider vinegar gives quite a different flavour. Malt vinegars can be either white or brown. The colour gives no indication at all as to the strength because caramel is used to colour the brown. A white malt vinegar can be used to advantage if you want a pickle or chutney to have a light colour.

The acidity of vinegar draws out and keeps the flavours of herbs and spices. Bottles of flavoured vinegars give zest and variety to salads and other dishes. You can make chilli, garlic, shallot, tarragon and many other herb vinegars. Flowers and fruit can also be steeped in vinegar. Lavender and rose are very fragrant. Blackberry or raspberry vinegar make delicious sauces to serve with plain boiled puddings; or they can be used for sore throats as they were in grandmother's day.

Chilli Vinegar

1 *pint wine or malt vinegar*   1 *oz. chillies*

Put the chillies in a bottle, cover with the vinegar, screw down tightly. Leave for about 1 month, shaking from time to time.

Garlic Vinegar

1 *pint dark or light wine or malt vinegar*   1 *oz. finely chopped garlic*

FLAVOURED VINEGARS, CHUTNEYS AND PICKLES

Put the vinegar in a glass jar, add garlic. Leave for about 2 weeks, shaking the jar from time to time. Strain into bottles. Cork securely. Use as required.

Shallot Vinegar

Made as garlic vinegar but substitute 2 oz. minced shallots for the garlic.

Spiced Vinegar

1 *quart vinegar*	8 *black peppercorns*
¼ *oz. whole mace*	¼ *oz. whole allspice*
¼ *oz. cinamon bark*	¼ *oz. whole cloves*

Tie the spices up loosely in a small piece of scalded muslin. Put them in a pan, add the vinegar, bring it slowly to boiling point. Cover the pan and simmer for 6–7 minutes. Remove from heat. Leave uncovered for 2–3 hours, then remove the bag of spices. Bottle, and use as required.

It is better to use whole spices as powdered ones can make the vinegar murky.

If you are a person who looks well ahead, spiced vinegar is even better if the spices are left to macerate in the vinegar for at least 2 months. The flavour will be stronger.

Tarragon Vinegar

All herb vinegars must be made with herbs freshly picked just before they flower, when they have optimum strength. If you have to buy your herbs, make certain that they are really fresh. Wipe or wash them.

Half fill a glass jar with tarragon leaves, cover with the best wine vinegar, leave for at least 4 weeks, shaking the jar from time to time. Strain into a bottle, cork securely. A sprig of tarragon can be put into the bottle, if liked, and left.

Rose Vinegar

Highly scented rose petals picked early in the morning (or use violet petals instead)

white wine vinegar

Fill a glass jar half full with rose petals, cover with wine vinegar. Leave in a warm place for 2–3 weeks. Strain and bottle. Cork securely.

These flower vinegars used to be poured on a large folded white handkerchief and laid on the forehead of the lady of the house when she had a headache.

Raspberry Vinegar

Of the fruit vinegars I like raspberry best, but blackberry, blackcurrant and redcurrant can be made.

3 lb. raspberries
2 pints white wine vinegar

1 *lb. caster sugar to each* 1 *pint of juice*

This takes 3 days to make and 1 lb. raspberries is added each day. Hull and pick over 1 lb. raspberries, put them in a bowl, pour the vinegar over them, squash them with a wooden spoon to extract the juice. Leave for 24 hours. Strain off the liquid. Put second 1 lb. of raspberries in the bowl, pour the liquid on them, squash with a wooden spoon, leave for 24 hours. Repeat this process on the third day, i.e. strain off the liquid, add third 1 lb. of fruit and leave for 24 hours. Now strain the liquid through a jelly bag overnight. Measure it and add the required amount of sugar. Put on a low heat, stir until the sugar is dissolved. Boil gently for 12 minutes. Skim if necessary. Let it cool, then bottle. Cork securely. This makes a most refreshing drink with added soda water, or it can flavour many sweets, baked custards and omelettes. Best of all as a sauce with a boiled batter pudding; also very soothing for sore throats if diluted with water.

CHUTNEYS

INTRODUCTION

Chutney making is probably one of the easiest and most fascinating ways of preserving. There is no need to be precise, as there is in making jam, jelly or marmalade. There are so many varieties and what you put in, how hot or spicy it is, really depends on your taste. You want a sweet chutney, so you add more sugar; a hot one, spice it up.

Chutneys are a good way of using up a glut of green tomatoes or windfalls, such as apples, plums or crab apples; these all make a good basis. A chutney should be reasonably smooth and not have too large pieces of fruit or onion in it. Apples, onions, garlic, tomatoes, etc., should be finely cut up or put through a mincer.

One of the secrets of a good chutney is long slow cooking.

Any fruit or vegetables that need a lot of cooking, such as green tomatoes, apples and onions, can be cooked before the spices, sugar and vinegar are added. If sultanas, seedless raisins or chopped stem ginger are going to be used they can be added with the sugar. The change of texture is pleasant: a crisp piece of ginger or a plumped up sultana please the palate. When whole spices are used, they should be tied up in a muslin bag and taken out when the chutney is put into the jars.

GENERAL HINTS FOR CHUTNEY MAKING (AND PICKLES)

Use the best-quality vinegar. Wine vinegar gives a more delicate taste. When salt is added, I like to use sea salt.

Use heavy pans made of stainless steel, aluminium, or chip-free enamel. Never use brass, iron or copper pans. Use a wooden spoon for stirring. This should be kept specially for chutneys as it becomes impregnated with the spicy smells.

It is important to use a nylon, hair or stainless steel sieve when sieving is necessary. Some metal gives an unpleasant metallic taste.

Aluminium pans should be thoroughly scoured before vinegar is used.

Never leave chutneys or pickles in the preserving pan overnight; acid attacks the metal.

Potting Pot the chutneys and pickles in warm jars. Cover when cold. The cover should be completely airtight in order to prevent evaporation of the vinegar, which is the chief preservative. Paper covers are not really suitable because then the chutney often shrinks and the top part dries up. If metal tops

FLAVOURED VINEGARS, CHUTNEYS AND PICKLES

are used the lacquer should be unbroken, and clean, fresh linings of cork or waxed cardboard put inside. If vinegar touches the metal it may corrode the lids. Melted paraffin wax is best (see page 29). Label jars and bottles, including the date.

Storing Most chutneys and pickles improve by being kept. In 6 months they are really mature. Check from time to time that they are keeping well.

POINTERS TO SUCCESS

- Use the best-quality vinegar.

- Cut up fruit and vegetables finely or mince them.

- Cook slowly and for a long time.

- Do not leave chutneys or pickles in the pan overnight.

- Make sure covers are completely airtight, to prevent evaporation.

Old Homestead Apple Chutney

3 *lb. apples*	½ *pint vinegar*
½ *lb. onions*	1 *dessertspoon salt*
2 *cloves of garlic*	1 *tablespoon ground ginger*
4 *oz. seedless raisins*	1 *tablespoon mustard seed*
1 *lb. brown sugar*	*a good pinch of ground chillies*

Put the washed apples, onions, raisins and garlic through the mincer. Put all the ingedients into the pan. Cook very slowly, stirring from time to time, until the mixture is thick. Pot and cover.

Banana and Apple Chutney

1–1½ lb. *under-ripe bananas*
1 lb. *sharp cooking apples*
¼ lb. *sultanas*
½ lb. *chopped onions*
2 *chopped cloves of garlic*
1 *teaspoon ground ginger*
1 *teaspoon salt*
1 *teaspoon mixed spice*
½ oz. *mustard seed*
½ *teaspoon turmeric*
½ *pint wine vinegar*

Peel, core and slice the apples. Put apples, onion, garlic, spices and vinegar in a heavy pan. Cook gently for about 20 minutes or until the apple has softened. Peel and slice the bananas, add them, cook and stir until the mixture is thick. Let the chutney cool, then pot and cover.

Chinese Sweet-Sour Mixed Fruit Chutney

1 lb. *plums (skinned and stoned)*
1 lb. *fresh ripe apricots*
1 *small pineapple (peeled, and hard centre core removed)*
½ *pint wine vinegar*
1 lb. *brown sugar (more or less, according to taste)*

Cut all the fruit up small. Put it in the preserving pan, add vinegar and some of the sugar. Bring to the boil, stir until sugar is dissolved. Taste and adjust sweetness and sourness; add more sugar if liked, or more vinegar. Simmer very slowly until the chutney is really thick (about 1½–2 hours). Stir frequently. Pot and seal. This goes especially well with duck or chicken (see pages 181, 177).

Mixed Fruit Chutney

This chutney can be made with windfall apples, pears, damsons and tomatoes – in fact you can blend any available fruit.

3 *lb. mixed fruit*	1 *teaspoon allspice*
4 *oz. dates*	½ *teaspoon ground cloves*
1 *lb. onions*	1 *teaspoon ground ginger*
2 *cloves of garlic*	1 *oz. mustard seed*
8 *oz. brown sugar*	1 *teaspoon ground pepper*
1 *heaped teaspoon salt*	1 *pint best-quality malt vinegar*

Wash, peel and core the fruit, remove any blemished pieces and stones. Cut the fruit, onions and garlic up very small, or put through the mincer if you like a very fine chutney. Mix fruit, onion, garlic, salt and sugar together. Add spices to the vinegar, simmer for 15 minutes. Put the fruit mixture into the pan, add the vinegar and cook gently until the mixture is really thick and well blended (this can take up to 2 hours). Stir from time to time to prevent the chutney from catching. Pot and cover.

Gooseberry Chutney

2 *lb. green gooseberries*	1½ *oz. ground ginger*
1 *lb. chopped onions*	½ *oz. salt*
¾ *lb. brown sugar*	½ *oz. mixed spice*
¼ *oz. mustard seed*	⅛ *oz. cayenne pepper*
4 *oz. sultanas*	1 *pint vinegar*

Top and tail the gooseberries, wash them. Put all the ingredients into the pan. Simmer gently, stirring from time to time, until the mixture is thick. Pot and cover.

Preserved Stem Ginger Chutney

1 *lb. preserved stem ginger (including syrup)*
2 *cloves of garlic*
3–4 *dry chillies*
½ *oz. fresh green ginger (obtainable from Indian stores)*
1 *teaspoon salt*
½ *pint wine vinegar*

Remove the pieces of ginger from the jar and chop them up small. Mince the garlic, chillies and peeled green ginger. Put the minced green ginger, garlic and chillies in the pan, add the vinegar and salt. Cook for 15–20 minutes until the green ginger is soft. Add the syrup and the cut-up ginger. Stir and cook until the chutney is really thick. Pot and cover.

Lime Chutney

1½ *lb. limes*
¼ *oz. dry chillies (more or less, to taste)*
3 *cloves garlic*
1 *oz. green ginger (see above)*
1½ *lb. brown sugar*
½ *lb. sultanas*
1 *oz. mustard seed*
¾ *pint vinegar*
¼ *oz. salt*

Wipe the limes, slice them finely, remove pips. Mince the chillies, garlic and ginger. Put all the ingredients in the preserving pan. Cook slowly until mixture is thick. Pot and cover.

Lemon Chutney

This can be made in the same way, using lemons instead of limes.

Green Mango Chutney

This is well worth making when you can buy the small green mangoes often on sale in Indian or Pakistani shops.

1 *lb. green mangoes*
salt
1 *lb. sugar*
¼ *lb. sultanas*
1 *oz. mustard seed*
3–4 *red chillies*
1 *garlic bulb*
1 *oz. finely sliced green ginger*
1 *pint vinegar*

Wipe the mangoes, peel and slice them, remove stones. Sprinkle them plentifully with salt. Leave for 24 hours in a warm place. Bruise the sliced mangoes; this helps to soften them; they are very hard when green and unripe. Peel and chop garlic. Add sugar, sultanas, mustard seed, garlic and ginger to the vinegar. Heat and stir until the sugar is dissolved, then simmer until vinegar mixture is syrupy. Add the sliced mangoes, cook until they are tender. Pot and cover.

Siamese Peach Chutney

3 lb. small peasants
1 finely chopped lemon (including peel, pips removed)
2 crushed, finely chopped cloves of garlic
½ lb. seedless raisins
3 tablespoons chopped stem or crystallised ginger
1 dessertspoon salt
1 teaspoon cayenne pepper (less if you do not a like a very hot chutney)
1½ pints cider vinegar
1 chopped, seeded green pimiento
1 lb. brown sugar

Peel the peaches, cut them in half, remove stones, chop coarsely. Mix all the ingredients together, put them in a pan. Cook very slowly, stirring frequently, until the chutney is really thick. Pot and cover.

Pear and Lemon Chutney

3 lb. just-ripe stewing pears
4–6 shallots
3 cloves of garlic
1 large smooth-skinned lemon
4 oz. sultanas)
4 oz. seedless raisins
4 oz. chopped stem ginger
1 teaspoon turmeric
1 teaspoon cinnamon
1 teaspoon pepper
1 teaspoon salt
½ teaspoon ground coriander
1 lb. brown sugar
1 pint red wine vinegar

Peel and core the pears and cut up into small dice. Chop the shallots. Crush and chop the garlic very fine. Slice the lemon, including the peel; chop it up small, discard pips. Put all the dry ingredients into a heavy saucepan, add the vinegar, bring slowly to simmering point, stirring frequently. Cook until fruit is quite soft and mixture thick. Pot and cover.

Plum Chutney

2 *lb. stoned plums*	1 *oz. ground ginger*
½ *lb. brown sugar*	1 *oz. salt*
1 *pint vinegar*	½ *oz. ground pepper*
1 *oz. finely chopped garlic*	1 *lb. sultanas or seedless raisins*

Put plums, vinegar and sugar in a preserving pan. Simmer until the plums are quite tender. Add the garlic, ginger, salt, pepper, and sultanas or raisins. Cook slowly, stirring occasionally until the mixture is very thick. Pot and cover.

PICKLES

BEST MONTHS FOR PICKLING VEGETABLES

All these vegetables should be young.

Beetroot	July, August
Cauliflower	July, August
Chillies	end of July, August
Field Mushrooms	September (for ketchups)
French Beans	July
Gherkins	middle of July, August
Onions	middle of July, August
Red Cabbage	August
Shallots	late June to late September
White Cabbage	September, October

Pickled Beetroot

Choose beetroots of an equal size and when they are young. Wash them carefully so that the skins are unbroken. Put in boiling salted water, simmer gently until they are cooked (this may take 1½–2 hours, according to size). When they are cooked the outside skin will come off easily. Let them cool, peel them and slice into circles. Pack into wide-mouthed jars and cover with cold spiced vinegar (see page 153). Or the beetroot can be cubed, packed in jars rather loosely and covered with boiling spiced vinegar. Cover.

Pickled Red Cabbage

Choose a young, firm, well-coloured cabbage. Remove the coarse outside leaves and white stalks. Shred it finely. Put it in a large basin, with layers of salt. Leave for 24 hours. Drain the cabbage and press out any liquid, rinse thoroughly. Pack loosely into wide-mouthed jars, cover with cold spiced vinegar (see page 153). This pickle is ready in a week, as it should be eaten when it is crisp. After 2–3 months it becomes too soft and no longer crunchy.

Cherries in Spiced Vinegar

2 lb. firm-fleshed, just-ripe cherries   *1 lb. sugar*

FOR THE SPICED VINEGAR

½ pint red wine vinegar   *¼ oz. coriander seeds*
1 bay leaf   *¼ oz. cardamom seeds*
¼ oz. whole allspice   *small piece of cinnamon bark*

Tie the spices and bay leaf in a muslin bag. Bring the vinegar slowly to the boil, add the spices, leave to infuse for 2–3 hours.

Dissolve the sugar in the vinegar, simmer until it thickens. Pack the cherries into jars, pour the boiling vinegar in. Seal. Leave to mature for 2 months. Serve with meat, game and poultry.

Pickled Indian Corn

This is well worth making if you can get really young immature corn cobs, no bigger than your middle finger.

young corn cobs *white peppercorns*
bay leaves *white wine vinegar*

Remove the green sheath leaves from the cobs. Pack them into stumpy wide-mouthed jars. Pack them alternately, with the tip of one cob pointing to the bottom of the jar and the next one towards the top and so on. Add a small bay leaf and a few peppercorns to each jar. Bring the vinegar to the boil, pour it over the cobs, completely filling the pots. Leave to cool, then cover. Serve with hors d'oeuvre or cold meat. If you are unable to get young corn, pickled corn is available in some delicatessen shops and supermarkets.

Pickled Damsons

4 *lb. damsons* 6 *cloves*
2 *lb. Barbados sugar* 12 *whole allspice berries*
1 *oz. bruised root ginger* 1 *pint vinegar*
1 *stick of cinnamon*

Tie the spices in a muslin bag. Put the vinegar and sugar in a heavy preserving pan, add the spices, bring slowly to the boil. Stir until sugar is dissolved. Simmer until vinegar has thickened and is syrupy. Wipe the damsons, prick each one with a silver or stainless steel fork. Put them in a large basin, pour the boiling vinegar and sugar on them. Leave for 48 hours. Strain off the vinegar, bring to the boil, add the damsons, bring to the boil, then remove from the heat immediately. Remove bag of spices, then remove the fruit with a perforated spoon. Pack it into jars, pour the vinegar over, cover at once. Leave for at least 2 months before using.

Very good with cold meats.

Peaches and pears can be pickled like this.

Pickled Dates

2–3 boxes juicy dates
1–1½ pints vinegar
12 peppercorns
10 cloves

a piece of cinnamon
1 teaspoon salt to each 1 pint of vinegar

Tie the spices in a muslin bag, add them to the vinegar and salt. Slit the dates down one side carefully, remove the stones but keep the dates whole. Pack them in a wide-mouthed jar. Boil up the vinegar with the spices and salt. Pour it over the dates, leave uncovered until they are cool, then cover securely. Leave for 1 month before using. These can be served with cold meat and curries, or in cream cheese sandwiches or salads.

Sweet and Sour Pickled Gherkins

Choose small gherkins as they fit into the jars more easily.

3–4 lb. gherkins	*1–1½ pints spiced vinegar (see page 153)*
2–3 oz. coarse salt	*2 oz. sugar*

Wipe the gherkins, put them in a large bowl, cover with salt and leave them overnight. The next day rinse and drain them well. Pack them into wide-mouthed jars. Add the sugar to the vinegar, heat and stir to dissolve, bring to the boil, pour over the gherkins. Leave for 24 hours. Strain off the vinegar, bring it to the boil again, pour it over the gherkins. This reheating of the vinegar and pouring it on the gherkins increases the green colour. The gherkins should be completely covered with vinegar; if necessary add more boiling spiced vinegar. Cover securely. Leave for 1 month before using.

Lime Pickle

1 lb. fresh green limes (about 6–7)	*2 teaspoons powdered allspice*
1 teaspoon turmeric	*1 gill wine vinegar*
1–1½ teaspoons chilli powder	*3 oz. brown sugar*

Wipe the limes, halve them then cut each half into six wedges. Mix together the turmeric, chilli powder, allspice, vinegar and sugar; stir in the limes. Pack into small, wide-mouthed, sterilised jars. The fruit should be completely covered with the pickle. Cover. This pickle matures slowly and it should not be eaten until the limes have softened. After a few days you can taste the sauce and see if you need to add more sugar; it will depend very much on personal taste. This is one of the most fragrant and subtle pickles I know. It is a must with all curries.

Lemon Pickle

This is made in the same way, lemons being used instead of limes.

Mint Sauce

½ pint malt or wine vinegar *caster sugar to taste*
1 pint finely chopped fresh mint

Wash the mint, let it dry. Strip the leaves from the stems. Chop it finely. Add sugar to the vinegar, then bring it to the boil. Let it cool. Pack the chopped mint into small screw-top jars. The dark green jars some capers are packed in are especially suitable. Cover the mint completely with the vinegar.

Clear Mixed Pickle

brine (allow 1 tablespoon sea salt to each 1 pint of water)
3 lb. green tomatoes
1½ lb. shallots
1 medium-sized cauliflower
1 small firm white cabbage
1 cucumber
1 lb. young runner or French beans
2 pints white malt vinegar
½ lb. brown sugar
5–6 cloves
4 blades of mace
1 bay leaf and 1 chilli for each jar of pickles

Make the brine by boiling sea salt and water together. Allow to cool. Wipe the tomatoes, slice them. Peel the shallots. Break the cauliflower into small flowerets. Wash the cabbage and slice finely. Discard any coarse leaves. Wipe the cucumber, cube it. Wash the beans, break into 1 in. lengths. Put all the vegetables into a large bowl, cover with brine. Leave for 24 hours. Drain thoroughly. Pack into sterilised jars. Put 1 bay leaf and 1 chilli into each jar. Put the vinegar, sugar and spices in a pan, bring to the boil, simmer for 5 minutes. Strain, bring to boiling point again. Fill up the jars. Seal. Keep for a few weeks before using.

Pickled Nasturtium Seeds

The real caper – Capparis spinosa – grows on a bramble-like bush found in South Europe. Mock capers are the pickled seeds of our garden nasturtiums. Pick the seeds on a dry day.

nasturtium seeds　　　　*brine made by dissolving 2 oz. salt*
spiced vinegar　　　　　*to 1 pint water*

Wash the seeds and soak them in the brine for 24–48 hours. Rinse and drain them. Put them into small and, if possible, dark-coloured jars, pour in cold spiced vinegar, cover and leave for some time before using.

Piccalilli

This was called Pickles Piccadilly in a French book! The name piccalilli covers a class of pickle which is typically English. It is regarded overseas, like Worcestershire sauce, as characteristically British. These pickles can be bitingly sour, hot and pungent, or moderately sweet, but they all contain small

PRESERVING WITH VINEGAR AND SPICES

identifiable pieces of vegetable in a bright yellow sauce. They are easy to make and a useful standby for cold meals. The vegetables can be crisp or soft according to the length of time they are cooked; they should never be soft enough to break up easily.

4–5 lb. mixed vegetables (cauliflowers, shallots, cucumber, green tomatoes, marrow, French beans)

4 oz. coarse salt

FOR THE HOT DRESSING

2 pints white vinegar
6 chillies
8 oz. granulated sugar
2 oz. mustard flour

1 oz. turmeric
1 teaspoon ginger
2 level tablespoons cornflour

FOR THE SWEET DRESSING

2 pints white vinegar
10 oz. granulated sugar
1 oz. mustard flour

1 oz. turmeric
2 chillies
4 level tablespoons cornflour

Wash the vegetables. Dice marrow and cucumber, quarter tomatoes, separate cauliflower into flowerets, cut beans into 1 in. lengths, peel the shallots. Put them on a large dish, cover with salt. Leave for 24 hours. Drain and rinse.

Mix together sugar, mustard flour, turmeric and cornflour (and for the hot piccalilli add the ginger), dilute with a little of the vinegar, stir to a smooth paste. Heat the rest of the vinegar with the chillies; when it comes to the boil, add the prepared vegetables and simmer gently until the desired texture is reached. Remove the vegetables and pack them into sterilised jars. Now add the cornflour mixture to the vinegar, stir and cook for 3 minutes, pour it into the jars. Seal tightly.

Pickled Onions

small pickling onions or shallots
brine (2 oz. coarse salt to each 1 pint water)

1 pint brine to each 1 lb. onions or shallots
cold spiced vinegar (see page 153)

Dissolve the salt in the water. Put the onions (unpeeled) in the brine, leave them overnight. The next day peel the onions with a stainless steel knife (this prevents them discolouring) under cold running water. Put them back in the brine and leave for 2 days. Drain thoroughly. Put the onions into sterilised jars, cover with cold spiced vinegar. Cover and keep for at least 3–4 months before using.

Pimientos Preserved in Vinegar

Choose small pimientos, either red or yellow.

6–8 pimientos
water
½ pint wine vinegar

2–3 tablespoons sugar
1 teaspoon salt

Wipe the pimientos, split them carefully down one side. Remove the stalk, seeds and membranes and keep these. Pour boiling water over the pimientos, leave for 15–20 minutes to soften them. Add the stems and seeds, sugar and salt to the vinegar, bring to the boil, then boil for 10 minutes. Drain the pimientos, pack them neatly in a wide-mouthed jar, pour in the

Pineapple Pickle

1 16 oz. *tin of pineapple cubes*
½ *oz. mustard seed*
½ *oz. dry chillies*
2 *cloves of garlic*
½ *oz. green ginger*
1 *teaspoon turmeric*
1 *gill wine vinegar*
1 *teaspoon salt*
2 *blades of mace*

Drain the pineapple (the juice can be used for making fruit salad). Pound the mustard seed, chillies, garlic and ginger with a little of the vinegar. Put the pineapple in a pan, add the spices, salt and vinegar, bring to the boil, leave to cool, then pour into jars and cover. This goes particularly well with ham.

Rhubarb Pickle

1½ *lb. rhubarb*
2 *lb. onions*
1½ *lb. brown sugar*
½ *lb. sultanas*
2 *tablespoons golden syrup*
1 *tablespoon salt*
1 *tablespoon curry powder*
1 *tablespoon mustard seed*
1 *quart vinegar*
3 *oz. flour*
1 *tablespoon turmeric*
water

Wash the rhubarb and cut up into 1 in. lengths. Peel and chop the onions. Put all the ingredients (except flour, turmeric and water) into a heavy pan. Stir and cook until the sugar is dissolved. Boil for 1 hour. Mix the flour and turmeric together, mix to a smooth paste with cold water. Add it to the rhubarb mixture. Cook and stir for 3–4 minutes. Pot in warm jars, cover and label.

Tomato Ketchup

12 *lb. ripe tomatoes*
1 *lb. brown sugar*
1 *lb. chopped onions*
2 *chopped cloves of garlic*
12 *cloves*
2 *oz. sea salt*
¼ *saltspoon cayenne pepper*
1 *teaspoon cinnamon*
½ *teaspoon ground ginger*
1 *quart vinegar*

Chop the tomatoes coarsely. Put all the ingredients in a pan. Bring to the boil slowly, then simmer until the tomatoes and onions are really soft. Stir from time to time with a wooden spoon to prevent burning. Strain the mixture through a nylon sieve. Bottle and cork. This sauce keeps well for a long time.

Pickled Walnuts with Sweet Spiced Vinegar

One rarely, if ever, sees green walnuts on sale in the shops. If you have a tree in the garden or can get some, do pickle some. They are a must with underdone cold roast beef. Wear gloves when picking or handling green walnuts; the stain is almost impossible to remove. When I was a child, I was always fascinated by the way pickled walnuts turned from green to black. It seemed like magic, as oxidisation was unknown to me.

The walnuts must be used when they are really young and the shell has not yet begun to form inside the green husk. Each nut should be tested by pricking with a needle or silver fork. The shell begins to form about ¼ inch from the opposite end to the stalk. If the walnuts are not completely soft, do not use them. Cover them with brine (1 lb. coarse salt to 1 gallon of water). Leave them for 6–7 days, then change the brine and soak them again for 6–7 days. Remove them and let them drain well. Spread them on large plates or dishes and leave them until they oxidise and turn black. When they are really black, pack them into wide-mouthed sterilised jars and cover with spiced vinegar (see page 153). Or you can cover them with a sweet spiced vinegar, which I prefer.

SWEET SPICED VINEGAR

3 *pints vinegar*
1 *lb. brown sugar*
1 *teaspoon whole mixed spice*
1 *teaspoon black peppercorns*
5–6 *whole cloves*

Tie the spices in muslin, add the sugar and spices to the vinegar, bring to the boil and simmer for 10 minutes. Pack the walnuts into sterilised jars. Remove the spices from the vinegar, pour it into the jars. Cover and leave for at least a month to mature.

Water Melon Pickle

5–6 *lb. watermelon rind*
4 *tablespoons sea salt*
5 *lb. sugar*
1 *pint white wine vinegar*
1½ *tablespoons whole cloves*
6 *blades mace*
3 *sticks cinnamon*
a piece of crushed root ginger
water

Remove most of the pink flesh from the water melon, but leave a little on. Cut the rind into 2 in. chunks or triangular pieces. Weigh 5–6 lb. Put it in a large bowl, add salt and 4 quarts of cold water. Leave overnight. The next day drain and rinse well. Put it in a heavy pan, cover with water and simmer until the rind is tender (this will take from 45–60 minutes). The rind must always be covered with water. Add the sugar, and the spices tied in a muslin bag. Stir until sugar is dissolved. Boil quickly until rind looks transparent. Add vinegar, cook for 5 minutes. Remove spices, pack the pickle into sterilised jars, seal and store in a cool place for at least 2 weeks before using.

SAVOURY RECIPES USING CHUTNEY AND PICKLES

Beef Smoore with Peach Chutney

1 chopped crushed clove of garlic
olive oil for frying
2–2½ lb. braising steak (chuck or bladebone)
2 chopped medium-sized onions

1 pint brown stock
pepper and salt to taste
1–2 teaspoons hot curry paste (more if liked)
5 fluid oz. sour cream

Heat the oil, brown the garlic. Cube the meat, add, and fry until brown all over. Add the onions, cook until soft and golden. Add the stock, curry paste, pepper and salt to taste. Bring to the boil, then simmer until meat is tender (1½–2 hours); the liquid should have reduced by about half. Remove from heat. Stir in the sour cream; let it warm through but do not let it boil. Correct seasoning. Serve with plain boiled rice and peach chutney (see page 162).

Boeuf Gros Sel

This country dish from France is made with beef boiled with vegetables. It is quite delicious. It is served with gros sel (coarse sea salt) and cornichons (gherkins, see page 167). As it is excellent cold, with the broth served beforehand as soup, allow more than you need for one meal.

For 4–6 people allow:

3½–4 lb. flank or brisket without bone and as lean as possible
bouquet garni
(2–3 sprigs of parsley, sprig of thyme and a bay leaf)
1 clove
6 peppercorns
2 large onions, quartered

3 carrots quartered lengthways
1 small turnip, chopped
1 large leek, chopped
1 chopped stick of celery
potatoes scrubbed clean
1 teaspoon sea salt (the broth must not be too salty)
water

Put the meat in a heavy saucepan. Choose the smallest one you have into which the meat will fit comfortably. Just cover with cold water, add bouquet garni, peppercorns, salt, clove and all the vegetables except potatoes. Bring to boiling point, skim if necessary. Simmer gently for 3 hours. Add potatoes 1–1½ hours, according to size, before the meat is cooked.

Carve the meat, serve it with the vegetables, and also serve gros sel, cornichons, mustard and some of the broth in a sauceboat. The rest of the broth will be a good basis for a soup.

Cheese and Chutney Quiche

Serves 4–5

8 oz. shortcrust pastry (deep frozen or see Appendix, page 220)	3 oz. grated Gruyère cheese
	freshly ground black pepper
	pinch of salt
lightly beaten egg white	sprinkling of nutmeg
½ pint creamy milk	2 heaped tablespoons chutney
3 eggs	

Line a 7 in. tin or flan ring with pastry (see page 221). Prick it lightly; brush it over with the egg white (this prevents the pastry becoming soggy). Mix the milk, cheese, chutney, pepper, salt and nutmeg together. Beat the eggs well and mix them in. Threequarters fill the tin. Cook at 350°F for 25–30 minutes. Serve hot or cold.

Cheese and Chutney Spread

1 lb. cream cheese	1 teaspoon curry paste
3–4 tablespoons chutney	2 oz. chopped walnuts

Mix all the ingredients together. Leave overnight in the refrigerator or a cool place (this allows the flavour to develop). Serve spread on bread, crispbread or unsweetened biscuits.

Chicken Siamese Style with Coconut Cream and Sweet-Sour Chutney

1 chicken (4–5 lb.)   coconut cream

TO MAKE COCONUT CREAM

- 1 *large coconut (or 4 oz. desiccated coconut)*
- ½ *pint boiling water (for first extract)*
- ¾ *pint boiling water (for second extract)*
- 2 *tablespoons soy sauce*

If you are going to use a fresh coconut, crack it and pour off the coconut milk. Remove the nut from the hard fibrous shell, scrape off all the brown skin. Grate the white flesh into a bowl. Pour the ½ pint of boiling water over it. Leave for 15 minutes, strain, and put this first extract aside for the stuffing. To make the second extract, add the ¾ pint of boiling water, transfer to a saucepan, bring to the boil, remove from the heat and let it cool. Strain off the cream. Discard the grated coconut, as most of the flavour and goodness will have gone. This cream, or second extract, is used to cook the chicken.

FOR THE STUFFING

- 1 *finely chopped medium-sized onion*
- 2 *finely chopped, crushed, cloves of garlic*
- 4 *oz. pork sausagemeat*
- 2 *tablespoons chopped mint*
- 1 *scant teaspoon cinnamon*
- *pinch of salt*
- *freshly ground pepper*
- ¼ *teaspoon cayenne pepper*
- 3 *oz. uncooked rice*
- 2 *oz. finely chopped roasted peanuts*
- *first extract of coconut cream*
- *oil for frying*

Heat the oil in a large frying pan. Fry the onion and garlic until they have softened. Add the sausagemeat, mashing it as it cooks. Mix in the mint, cinnamon, salt, pepper, cayenne pepper, rice and peanuts. Cook and stir for 3–4 minutes. Add the coconut cream, stir to mix, simmer very gently until rice is tender and most of the coconut cream has been absorbed. If necessary add some of the second extract if the rice mixture becomes too dry. Let it cool. Stuff the chicken with it, then truss it. Add 2 tablespoons soy sauce to the second extract of coconut, put the bird in a saucepan, pour on the coconut cream, cover, cook gently for 1½–2 hours until chicken is tender. Serve with the liquid the bird was cooked in, and sweet-sour chutney (see page 158).

If preferred the chicken can be stuffed in the same way but roasted in the oven for 1½–2 hours. Serve with second extract of coconut cream flavoured with soy sauce, as gravy, and sweet-sour chutney.

Baked Chutney Cheese Rolls

6 *soft bread rolls*	1 *clove of garlic*
12 *thin slices of cheddar cheese*	2 *oz. melted butter*
(about the same size as the rolls)	*chutney*

Peel, chop and crush the garlic; add it to the melted butter. Cut the rolls in half; brush them over with the garlic butter. Spread chutney on top, then place a slice of cheese on each half roll. Arrange the rolls on an oven tray and bake in a moderate oven (350°F) until the rolls are crisp and the cheese lightly brown (about 10 minutes). Serve hot with a lettuce salad, gherkins and olives.

Connoisseur's Carp

Like many freshwater fish, carp have a slightly 'muddy' taste. To get rid of this, soak them in cold salted water for 3–4 hours, then wash them in vinegar and water, scale and gut them. Cooked the following way with a full-flavoured sauce they are delicious.

1 carp (weighing about 3–4 lb. for 3–4 people)
flour
equal quantity of butter and oil for shallow frying
equal quantity of water and port wine (enough to cover the fish)
1 large tablespoonful lemon pickle (see page 168)
1 tablespoon mushroom ketchup (see page 217)
pepper and salt
1 bay leaf
pinch of cayenne pepper
1 small chopped onion
4–5 cloves

Prepare the fish, dredge it with flour and fry it until brown in the hot butter and oil. Put the fish in a shallow pan, cover with water and port wine, add lemon pickle, mushroom ketchup, pepper, salt, bay leaf, cayenne pepper, onion and cloves. Bring slowly to the boil, reduce heat and cook gently until the fish is done, about 20–30 minutes. Remove the fish, keep it hot. Thicken the sauce with beurre manié (see page 223). Simmer it for 3–5 minutes. Strain the sauce over the fish. Serve with boiled potatoes.

Crab and Pickle Canapés

6–8 oz. deep-frozen crabmeat
lemon juice
4–5 finely chopped pickled onions
sweet chutney (see page 162)
pepper and salt
1–2 tablespoons mayonnaise
small lettuce leaves
rounds of buttered toast

Read instructions on pack or packet of crab. Let it thaw out. Flake it, add the lemon juice, pickled onions, pepper, salt, and

Roast Stuffed Duck with Sweet-Sour Chutney

1 *duck (4–5 lb.)*   1 *crushed clove garlic*

FOR THE STUFFING

1–2 oz. butter	1 *large piece of stem ginger, finely chopped*
finely chopped duck giblets	
1 *finely chopped onion*	2 *tablespoons soy sauce*
1 *finely chopped and crushed clove of garlic*	2 *oz. sliced mushrooms*
	6 *oz. uncooked rice*
freshly ground pepper	½ *pint warm stock*

Melt the butter, cook the giblets for about 5 minutes. Add the onion and garlic, stir and fry until onion is softened, then add mushrooms, ginger and soy sauce. Stir and cook for 2–3 minutes. Add pepper and rice, stir and cook over low heat, now add the warm stock, stir and cook until most of the liquid has been absorbed. Let it cool, stuff the duck loosely and truss it. Prick the skin all over; this allows the fat to run out so that the duck is less fat and the skin crisper. Rub the bird all over with crushed garlic. Cook at 325°F allowing 30 minutes per pound. Baste frequently. If the skin is not brown enough for your taste, step up the heat for the final 20–30 minutes. Serve with sweet-sour chutney and a green vegetable.

Eggs in Baked Potatoes with Chutney

Allow half a large potato and 1 egg per person. For 4:

2 *large baking potatoes*	*pepper and salt to taste*
1½–2 *oz. butter*	2 *tablespoons chutney*
1 *gill milk*	4 *eggs*

Scrub the potatoes thoroughly. Prick them all over with a fork; oil them (this keeps the skins from hardening). Bake at 325°F for about an hour. When the potatoes are cooked, remove them from the oven. Cut them in half lengthwise. Scoop out most of the inside, mash it with the butter, milk, pepper, salt and chutney. Replace it in the potato shells. Make an indentation in the centre. Break the eggs and slide one into each half. Season with pepper and salt, put them in a baking dish, cover and bake at 350°F until the eggs are set to your liking (roughly 15 minutes). Serve hot with chutney on the side.

Fish Cakes with Lemon Pickle

Serves 4

1 *lb. boned, skinned cooked fish* (*such as cod, herrings, smoked haddock*)	1–2 *tablespoons finely chopped or minced lemon pickle* (*see page* 168)
8 *oz. white breadcrumbs*	1 *tablespoon chopped parsley*
1 *oz. softened butter*	1 *slightly beaten egg for binding*
1 *minced onion*	*pepper and salt*

FOR COATING

beaten egg	*butter or fat for frying*
browned breadcrumbs	

Pound the fish in a mortar or liquidise it. Mix in the breadcrumbs, softened butter, onion, lemon pickle, parsley, pepper and salt. Bind with the egg. Shape into flat cakes. Brush over with the beaten egg, cover with breadcrumbs, fry in hot fat until brown on both sides. Serve with extra lemon pickle on the side.

Ham-Stuffed Marrow

Serves 4

- 1 *medium-size young marrow or 2 small ones*
- *freshly ground black pepper*
- ½ *teaspoon salt*
- 2 *tablespoons Barbados sugar*
- 8–10 *oz. minced ham*
- 1 *oz. fine white breadcrumbs*
- 1 *tablespoon chopped parsley*
- 1 *tablespoon finely chopped onion*
- 2 *heaped tablespoons chopped pickles or chutney*
- 2 *tablespoons tomato concentrate (diluted with a little hot water)*
- 2 *tablespoons melted butter*

Wipe the marrow; do not peel it. Cut it in half lengthwise, put it cut side down in a shallow fireproof dish, add about ½ in. water. Bake in a fairly hot oven (400°F) for 15–20 minutes or until the marrow is tender. Drain well, scoop out the centre; take care not to break the skin. Sprinkle the inside of the marrow halves with pepper, salt and sugar. Mix together the ham, breadcrumbs, parsley, onion, pickles or chutney, tomato concentrate and the scooped out marrow. (There should not be any seeds if you have chosen a young one.) Fill the marrow halves, brush over with melted butter. Bake a further 15–20 minutes at 400°F. Serve hot.

Piquant Stuffed Lamb Shoulder

To be served cold. Serves 6

1 *boned shoulder of lamb*	2 *tablespoons chopped gherkins*
3 *oz. rolled oats*	*(see page 167)*
1 *gill of milk*	1 *large, skinned, chopped tomato*
4 *finely chopped pickled onions*	1 *teaspoon oregano*
(see page 171)	*freshly ground pepper and salt*
1 *crushed clove of garlic*	1 *lightly beaten egg for binding*
1 *teaspoon grated lemon rind*	*pineapple rings, tomato halves and lettuce leaves for garnish*

Soak the rolled oats in milk for 15 minutes. Add onions, garlic, lemon rind, gherkins, tomato, oregano, pepper and salt. Bind with the egg. Spread this mixture evenly over the inside of the meat. Roll it up; tie or skewer it. Wrap the joint in greased foil. Bake in a moderate oven (350°F) for 1¾–2 hours. Remove foil after 1 hour so that the meat browns. When cooked, leave to cool. When cold, keep in the refrigerator overnight for eating the next day. Carve it vertically and serve garnished with pineapple rings, tomato halves and lettuce.

FLAVOURED VINEGARS, CHUTNEYS AND PICKLES

Baked Meat Loaf

Chutney gives this dish a different, piquant taste.
Serves 4–5

¾ lb. finely minced lean beef
¾ lb. finely minced veal
2 finely chopped bacon rashers
4–5 oz. fine white breadcrumbs
extra breadcrumbs for coating baking dish
1 small finely chopped onion
1 crushed clove of garlic

1 tablespoon chopped parsley
1 teaspoon ground coriander
plenty of freshly ground pepper
1 teaspoon salt
3 tablespoons chutney
½ pint tomato juice
1 lightly beaten egg to bind
butter

Mix minced meat, bacon, breadcrumbs, onion, garlic, parsley, coriander, pepper, salt and chutney well together. Stir in tomato juice, mix in the beaten egg. Well butter a loaf tin or fireproof dish, sprinkle plentifully with breadcrumbs, fill with the meat mixture. Bake in a moderate oven 1–1¼ hours. Serve hot, with a green vegetable.

Pickleburgers

Serves 4–5

1 lb. minced beef
1 lb. minced pork
2 eggs
2 tablespoons soft breadcrumbs
pepper and salt

1 finely chopped onion
1 finely chopped clove of garlic
2 tablespoons chopped pickle

Mix all the ingredients, except the pickle, well together. Shape the meat into flat cakes. Spread half of them with the pickle; top with the rest of the meat. Press the edges well together so that the pickle does not extrude. Grill until brown on both sides. Serve in hamburger rolls or with vegetables.

Walnut Sauce

This sauce goes well with fish and meat. It brightens up boiled or baked cod and hake. Excellent with a lamb stew.

¾ pint fish or meat stock (depending on what it is to be served with)
2 oz. butter
2 small finely chopped onions
1½ oz. flour
pepper and salt to taste
4 finely chopped pickled walnuts (see page 173)
1 tablespoon vinegar from pickled walnuts

Melt the butter, add the onions, fry them until they are brown. Add the flour; blend it in, then gradually add the stock; stir until it is smooth. Cook gently for 15–20 minutes. Season to taste. Add the walnut vinegar and the chopped pickled walnuts. Remove from the heat and serve at once.

Welsh Rarebit with Pickles

A snack for 4

1 gill of beer
2 tablespoons chopped mixed pickles (see page 168)
6 oz. grated mousetrap cheese
4 slices hot buttered toast

Put the beer, pickles and cheese in a heavy pan. Heat gently, stirring until the cheese is melted and well blended. Taste for seasoning. If liked, pepper and Worcestershire sauce may be added; this really depends on personal taste and on how 'tasty' the cheese is. Pile on the hot buttered toast. It may be popped under a hot grill for a minute or so to brown the top.

SWEET RECIPES

Boiled Batter Pudding with Raspberry Vinegar

Popular in the nineteenth century, the boiled pudding deserves to be revived. Properly made it is nourishing and feather light – not at all soggy. The Victorians liked to boil them in a cloth and not a basin, they thought there was more room for them to 'swell'.

They can be served sprinkled with caster sugar and raspberry vinegar, (or with warmed redcurrant or blackcurrant jelly).

4 *eggs*	8 *oz. plain flour*
1 *pint milk*	*small pinch of salt*

Beat the eggs thoroughly, add ½ pint of milk to them, strain. Sift flour and salt into a basin, add the egg and milk slowly, Beat well for about 5 minutes, then gradually add the other ½ pint of milk, stirring all the time. Cover, and leave for 30 minutes. Pour the batter into a greased pudding basin; leave room for the pudding to rise. Cover with a greased paper, boil gently for 1 hour and 10 minutes. Turn it out onto a hot dish.

Quickly but gently cut deep parallel gashes about 1 inch apart on top, then do the same at right angles. Sprinkle plentifully with caster sugar and pour raspberry vinegar over. (Or warm a small jar of redcurrant or blackcurrant jelly and pour it over the top.) Serve at once.

If you prefer to boil the pudding in a cloth, choose thick white material, scald it and cover it thickly with flour. Put the cloth in a basin. Beat the batter well, pour it in, tie up securely and plunge the pudding into boiling water. As soon as it comes back to the boil, reduce heat and boil gently. If a saucer is put on the bottom of the saucepan the pudding will not stick. The boiling water should completely cover the pudding.

Spicy Watermelon Slices

Serve for tea or topped with whipped cream as a dessert.

8 oz. plain flour
1 teaspoon bicarbonate of soda
2 teaspoons cinnamon
½ teaspoon nutmeg
4 oz. butter

6 oz. brown sugar
2 eggs
5 fluid oz. sour cream
1 cup watermelon pickle (see page 174)

Sift flour, bicarbonate of soda, cinnamon and nutmeg together. Cream butter and sugar well together. Add the eggs, one at a time, beating in well. Add the dry ingredients alternately with the sour cream, then add the finely chopped, drained, watermelon pickle. Grease and lightly flour a shallow tin approximately 9 in. × 13 in. Pour in the mixture, bake for 25–30 minutes in a moderate oven (350°F). Cut into slices when cold.

Preserving by Drying

☙

Herbs, Flowers, Leaves and Stalks
*Drying Herbs, Using Dried Herbs and
Making Tisanes (Infusions)*

Herbs, Flowers, Leaves and Stalks

HERBS

Introduction
Best Months for Drying Herbs
Dried Herbs in the Kitchen

FLOWERS, LEAVES AND STALKS

Tisanes (Infusions)

Chamomile (Camomille)
Cherry Stalks (Queues de Cerises)

Elderflowers (Sureau)
Lime Flowers (Tilleul)
Mint (Menthe)
Rosemary (Romarin)
Vervain (Verveine)

SOME RECIPES USING HERBS

Poulet à l'Estragon (Tarragon Chicken with Suprême Sauce)

Pomegranate Soup with Meat Balls
Béarnaise Sauce

HERBS

INTRODUCTION

Herbs, fresh in season and dried for winter, add quite a lot to cooking. It is well worth the little trouble it takes to preserve them. Their fragrance is most evocative, the smell of thyme and fennel immediately transports me back to Provence. Mint must always remind the English of new potatoes, fresh garden peas and roast lamb.

They should be gathered on a dry day when they are in their prime, just before they flower. They should be washed and then dried in a very cool oven for about 1 hour or tied up loosely and covered with muslin, to protect them from dust and flies, and hung up in an airy room. Some people like to dip them in boiling water before drying them, and this does help to keep them a brighter green. They should be dried until they are brittle enough to be powdered or pulverised. Or dried leaves and sprigs such as rosemary, thyme and tarragon can be stored whole in jars.

BEST MONTHS FOR DRYING HERBS

Basil	August
Bay leaves	June, July
Chervil	May, June, July
Fennel	May, June, July
Marjoram	July
Mint	end of June, July
Parsley	May, June, July
Rosemary	May, June
Sage	August, September
Summer Savory	end of July, August
Tarragon	June, July, August
Thyme	end of July, August

DRIED HERBS IN THE KITCHEN

Bouquet Garni A sprig of thyme, parsley and a bay leaf tied together and added to soups, stews, casseroles, etc. Should be removed before dish is served.

Basil (Sweet and Bush) Used in soups, especially Soup au Pistou, stews, sauces. Has an affinity with tomatoes. Traditional flavour for Turtle Soup. Remains very aromatic when dried.

Bay Leaves Part of a bouquet garni. Used for flavouring savoury dishes, court bouillons, marinades. In Victorian times added to custards, blancmanges.

Chervil May be used instead of parsley.

Fennel Goes magnificently with fish.

Marjoram Added to soups, omelettes. Good with white fish, poultry and roast pork.

Mint A pinch of dried mint can be added to the water in which new potatoes and green peas are cooked, when fresh mint is not available. Makes mint sauce (see page 168).

Parsley Dried parsley can be used instead of fresh for sauces, stews, casseroles and with egg dishes.

Rosemary Goes well with pork and lamb. Use only a little as it is overpowering if used excessively.

Sage Goes particularly well with roast pork and veal. Can flavour rissoles.

Savory Used in stuffings, added to hamburgers. The French like it with trout. It may be added to marinades.

Tarragon Good with tomatoes, eggs, chicken (see Poulet à l'Estragon, page 195). Makes Sauce Tartare and Béarnaise Sauce (see page 197). Can be added to fish aspics and to vinegar to make tarragon vinegar (see page 153).

Thyme Part of a bouquet garni.

FLOWERS, LEAVES AND STALKS

Tisanes
(Infusions)

The French dry many flowers, leaves and stalks, then infuse them in a teapot with boiling water for 4–5 minutes and sip them for pleasure or their curative qualities.

The plants should be picked on a dry day when there is no dew on them and dried, in the same way as herbs, in a very slow oven – on no account let them char. Or they can be spread on paper and left to dry away from strong sunlight. If they are at all dusty, they must be gently washed or wiped. When they are dry, pack them into jars.

When the infusion is made it is strained into cups. Sugar may be added if liked, but never milk. Sometimes two flavours are combined: lime flowers and mint for example.

The most popular tisanes are:–

Chamomile (Camomille)   1 dessertspoon of the dried flowers infused in 1 pint of boiling water. Good for the digestion. A few of the dried flowers added to a hot bath is very refreshing.
Cherry Stalks (Queues de Cerises)   In the north of France the housewife saves and dries cherry stalks for stubborn coughs and colds. 15–20 stalks infused in 1 pint of boiling water.
Elderflowers (Sureau)   3 teaspoons to 1 pint of boiling water. Has the flavour of muscat grapes. The dried flowers can be added to Indian tea in the proportion of 1 part elderflowers to 3 parts tea to make a most fragrant brew, rather like the best Darjeeling.

Lime Flowers (Tilleul)   It is a lovely sight to see great hillocks of lime flowers drying in the open in the south of France. The smell is unforgettable. Both the flowers and bracts are dried. 1 dessertspoon infused in 1 pint of boiling water. Its honey flavour is most attractive. It soothes the nerves and induces sleep. A flower or two can be added to baked or boiled custards to flavour them.

Mint (Menthe)   There are many kinds of mint, but the one called peppermint makes the best tea (not the spearmint which is the best mint for sauce). Infuse a few leaves in 1 pint of boiling water. Good for the digestion.

Rosemary (Romarin)   Infuse a few of the spiky leaves in a pint of boiling water. Good for a nervous headache and it is said to improve a bad memory!

Vervain (Verveine)   A few leaves infused in 1 pint of boiling water is good for the digestion. (This wild plant has nothing to do with the garden Verbena which is very perfumed and used in scents and soaps.)

SOME RECIPES USING HERBS

Poulet à L'Estragon
(Tarragon Chicken with Suprême Sauce)

Serves 4

3½–4 lb. jointed chicken   *1 teaspoon dried tarragon*
1 quart strong white stock

Poach the chicken in the stock with the added tarragon. When it is cooked (about 1–1½ hours), keep it hot while you make the sauce.

FOR THE SUPRÊME SAUCE

1½ *pints of the chicken stock*	*pepper and salt to taste*
2½ *oz. butter plus an extra 1 oz.*	1 *teaspoon lemon juice (or to taste)*
2 *oz. flour*	1½ *tablespoons chopped dried tarragon (soaked in a little of the stock)*
2 *tablespoons double cream*	
3 *egg yolks*	

Melt the butter, stir in the flour, do not let it colour. Cook for 3–4 minutes, stirring all the time. Add the stock, stir it in until the sauce is smooth. Let it cook slowly for 20 minutes. Now make the liaison. Beat the egg yolks and cream lightly together, add this to the sauce, stir gently and cook over a low heat until the egg yolks thicken the sauce. Do not let it boil or the sauce may curdle. Gradually add small pieces of butter from the extra 1 oz., stirring them in until they have melted. Add the lemon juice and the tarragon. Correct the seasoning. Arrange the chicken on a serving dish, and cover with the sauce. Serve with boiled rice.

Pomegranate Soup with Meat Balls

Serves 4

FOR THE MEAT BALLS

½ *lb. minced lean beef*	*a good pinch of cinnamon*
1 *small minced onion*	*lightly beaten egg for binding*
pepper and salt	*fat for frying*

DRYING HERBS AND USING DRIED HERBS

FOR THE SOUP

1½ pints chicken stock
2 oz. rice
½ lb. chopped spinach
2 tablespoons chopped parsley
4–5 chopped spring onions
   (including the green part)
½ pint pomegranate juice
   about 4–5 depending on their
   juiciness, or use pomegranate
   syrup, see page 144)
freshly ground pepper
sugar to taste
lemon juice to taste
pinch of cinnamon
2 tablespoons dried mint
   (see page 192)

Make the meat balls first. The onion must be finely minced or chopped; if not, it drops out of the meat balls. Mix meat and seasonings well together. Bind with the lightly beaten egg. Form into small balls. Fry until brown all over in hot fat.

Cook the rice in the chicken stock for 10 minutes. Add the chopped spinach, parsley and onions, pepper and cinnamon. Cook for 15 minutes. Squeeze the pomegranates. This is quite easily done with a large lemon squeezer. Or the fruit can be cut in half, and the pips scooped out and liquidised, then strained. Add the juice and the meat balls. Cook for 15–20 minutes. Correct the seasoning; if the pomegranates make the soup too sharp or too sweet, counteract this with lemon juice or sugar. Sprinkle in the chopped mint just before serving.

Béarnaise Sauce

3 fluid oz. tarragon vinegar (see
   page 153)
1 chopped shallot
1 small, crushed clove of garlic
sprig of parsley
3 egg yolks
1 tablespoon cold water
coarsely ground white pepper
2 tablespoons dried chopped tarragon (see page 192)
2–3 oz. butter
salt

Put the tarragon vinegar into a small heavy saucepan, add the shallot and garlic. Let the vinegar reduce slowly over a low heat until there is about 1 large tablespoon. Strain it. Put the egg yolks and the tablespoon of water into the cold vinegar. Add pepper, chopped tarragon, butter and salt to taste. Cook it in a double saucepan or in a basin which will fit over a saucepan of cold water. Heat gently, stirring constantly, until the sauce has thickened and is creamy. Correct the seasoning. This sauce goes well with egg dishes and grilled steak.

Preserving With Alcohol

Making and Using Liqueurs and
Wine Infusions

Preserving With Alcohol

Introduction
Pointers to Success

Angel's Liqueur
Apricots in Sherry
Blackcurrant Liqueur
Blackcurrant Rum
The Cardinal's Ghost (Kardinalgeist)
Cherry Brandy
Chilly Sherry
Clove Carnation Ratafia

La Confiture de Vieux Garçons (Bachelors' Jam)
Juniper Liqueur
Noyau Liqueur
Orange Brandy
Peaches in Brandy
Raspberry Ratafia
Rum Pot

ADDITIONAL RECIPES

Ham and Apricot Rolls

Cambridge Apricot Tart
Ginger Apricot Bavarois

PRESERVING WITH ALCOHOL

INTRODUCTION

Preserving with alcohol is really simple because there is nothing to go wrong. To make liqueurs all one needs is alcohol, sugar and either fruit, plant stems or nuts.

PRESERVING WITH ALCOHOL

Some of one's duty-free ration brought back from holidays can be used in this way. Even if you buy your spirits in England, your liqueurs will be cheaper than those on sale here and as the result is your own concoction, it is much more fun to drink.

When the French housewife makes her liqueurs she often calls them ratafias. When she does not use brandy she buys the cheaper eau-de-vie at 40°.

There are really no hard and fast rules as to what alcohol one uses: it may be brandy, gin, whisky or rum. If you ever get a white spirit of 70° it can be cut with $\frac{1}{3}$ of distilled water or a sugar syrup. The amount of fruit does not matter, the quantity of sugar is very much a matter of taste. Extra fruit, sugar and alcohol can be added as and when desired.

These home-made liqueurs can be used in many different ways. They can be added to fruit salads, to sauces for ice creams and puddings, or drunk as liqueurs in thimble-sized glasses (for economy's sake). If you make cherry brandy or cherry whisky, the cherries can be eaten separately and the liquid served as a liqueur. Remember that these cherries can be extremely alcoholic and even the hardiest of topers can get drunk if he eats too many.

POINTERS TO SUCCESS

○ Use good fruit

○ Use good alcohol

○ Offer to your friends

Angel's Liqueur

Angelica – popular from Finland to France – has a strong and very pleasant flavour. (It is one of the herbs used in making Chartreuse). This is an unusual and delicious digestive.

1 *bottle of vodka (or white alcohol)*	*easy to buy, but they are on sale in some specialist shops)*
½ *lb. angelica stems*	6 *cardamom seeds*
4–5 *blanched and chopped bitter almonds (these are not always*	¼ *pint water*
	½ *lb. sugar (or to taste)*

Wash and scrape the angelica stalks. Crush the cardamom seeds. Put the angelica, bitter almonds and cardamoms in a jar, pour in the vodka. Stopper securely. Leave to macerate for at least 6 weeks. Shake the jar occasionally. Make a syrup with the water and sugar, let it boil for 10 minutes. Allow to cool, then add it to the liqueur. Leave for a further month, then filter and bottle. It is now ready for use, but it improves the longer it is kept. Sometimes it throws a deposit; if it does, carefully refilter it.

Apricots in Sherry

dried stoned apricots   *sweet sherry (Cyprus does very well)*

If possible use whole dried apricots; otherwise, apricot halves. Wash them, pack them into a kilner jar, fill up with sherry. As the apricots soften and absorb the liquid, add more sherry from time to time. Leave for at least 3 months before using.

Apricots in sherry are very versatile and may be added to both savoury and sweet dishes. They are super with ham (see page 211), can be added to fruit salads, and make Ginger Apricot Bavarois (see page 212).

Blackcurrant Liqueur

equal quantity of blackcurrants and sugar
brandy
a few of the tiny blackcurrant leaves (they are very perfumed)

Remove the stalks from the blackcurrants, wash the leaves. Put fruit, leaves, sugar in a bowl. Mash with a wooden spoon. Add brandy, stir to mix. Pour into a wide-mouthed jar. Cover tightly. Leave for 2 months. Strain off the liquid. Put the fruit in a clean white cloth and squeeze out all the juice. Filter through paper; bottle and stopper.

Perfectionists start making this in the spring. They marinate the tiny leaf buds (the burgeon) of the blackcurrant bush in the alcohol they will eventually use for their liqueur.

Blackcurrant Rum

1½ lb. blackcurrants
1½ lb. loaf or granulated sugar
rum

Stalk the blackcurrants, rinse them in cold water, drain. Put them in a crock or wide-mouthed jar, add the sugar and pour the rum on top. Leave for 2–3 months, shaking the jar three or four times a week to dissolve the sugar.

The Cardinal's Ghost
(Kardinalgeist)

This orange-flavoured 'spirit' can be added to fruit salads, sauces and many drinks, including the famous German Bowle.

2 *Seville oranges*
2 *thin-skinned sweet oranges*
1–1½ *in. piece of cinnamon bark*
4 *oz. preserving sugar*
1 *pint rum or brandy*

Scrub the oranges clean. Peel them very thinly; be careful not to leave any white pith on the zest. Cut the peel into matchstick strips, put them in a wide-mouthed jar. Add the sugar and cinnamon. Pour in the rum or brandy. Squeeze the oranges, strain the juice into the jar. Cover and leave for 4–6 weeks. Shake the jar from time to time to help dissolve the sugar. Strain into scrupulously clean bottles, cork tightly.

FOR THE BOWLE

Take equal quantities of chilled Rhine or Moselle wine and iced soda water, add a small wineglass of Cardinal's Ghost, or to taste. Mix thoroughly. Decorate with slices of peach, apple or orange. Sliced cucumber or borage leaves may be added too if liked.

Cherry Brandy

1 *lb. just-ripe black cherries*
¾ *lb. sugar*
brandy

Wipe the cherries, snip off the stalks, leaving about 1 in. Prick each cherry once or twice with a silver fork or stainless steel skewer. Put them in a wide-mouthed jar. A clove and a piece of cinnamon bark may be added or a few bitter almonds. Add the sugar and cover with as much brandy as you can spare. Leave for 2–3 months, shaking the jar three or four times a week to dissolve the sugar.

Eat the cherries separately. Serve the brandy in small liqueur glasses.

Chilli Sherry

In some army Messes soup was always served with chilli sherry sprinkled from small cut glass bottles.

small, fresh red chillies *sherry*

Wipe the chillies and remove the stalks. Put the chillies in a small jar, cover with a medium-dry sherry. Leave for at least 1 month before using. Serve in a small sprinkler-top bottle.

Clove Carnation Ratafia

Pick dark-red clove carnations at the height of their perfection. Remove the petals one by one, wipe if necessary.

½ lb. carnation petals *½ lb. granulated sugar*
1 clove *1 gill water*
1–1½ in. piece of cinnamon bark *brandy*

Put the petals, clove and cinnamon in a jar, and cover with brandy. Leave for 1 month. Strain and filter through paper.

Dissolve the sugar in the water, bring to the boil and boil for

10 minutes. Let it cool, then strain it into the liqueur. Bottle and stopper tightly.

Violets can be treated in the same way. Be sure to use scented ones and omit the clove and cinnamon. This will taste like Parfait d'Amour if left to mature.

La Confiture de Vieux Garçons
(Bachelors' Jam)

This delightful French way of preserving fruit is not a jam at all. It is a combination of sugar and alcohol into which you plunge different fruits at the peak of their perfection as they come into season. The first layer is usually strawberries, then come cherries, raspberries, peaches, pears, apricots and the last layer, which is invariably of grapes both white and black.

As this bachelors' joy is left to mature the alcohol takes on colour and flavour and the fruit becomes impregnated. The result is a liqueur and intoxicated fruit which can be served with ice cream or put into fruit salads.

alcohol (this can be brandy, rum, eau-de-vie or even whisky)
granulated sugar 1 lb. sugar to each 1 lb. of fruit (this can be added each time fresh fruit is put into the jar)
fruit

A stone crock should be used if possible, failing this a large glass jar.

Strawberries Choose large, just-ripe strawberries. Hull and wipe them, put them whole in the crock or jar.
Cherries Choose sweet ones, wipe them, prick them, remove

stalks and stones too if you like. Put them on top of the strawberries.

Raspberries Choose large, perfect ones. Hull and wipe if necessary.

Apricots Choose small really ripe ones, wipe them, remove stones, cut in half.

Peaches Peel the peaches, cut them into large slices, remove stones.

Greengages Choose ripe ones, wipe them, remove stones, cut in half.

Pears Choose just-ripe pears; if they are soft they will cloud the 'jam'. Peel them, remove core, cut into thick slices.

Grapes Choose sweet ones, wash, drain and remove pips.

When the first lot of fruit has been put in the crock, add the same weight of sugar and cover with the alcohol. Tie down or stopper securely so that there is no evaporation. As each fresh batch of fruit is added, add the same amount of sugar and make sure that the fruit is covered with spirit. Add more of the same kind of alcohol if necessary.

Small jars filled with a mixture of fruits in their liquor make very handsome Christmas presents.

Juniper Liqueur

1 *oz. crushed juniper berries*
slices of lemon
8 *oz. granulated sugar* (*more or less, according to taste*)

1 *gill water*
about ½ pint gin

Macerate the juniper berries in the gin, with the lemon slices. Leave for 1 week. Heat the water, add the sugar, stir to dissolve, bring to the boil. Let it cool, strain it into the gin. Leave for 4–5 weeks. Strain through filter papers. Bottle and stopper tightly.

Noyau Liqueur

apricot, peach and cherry stones
brandy
sugar (allow the same quantity of sugar as the weight of the fruit stones)
½ gill water to 4 oz. sugar

Put the stones in a small, wide-mouthed jar. Cover with brandy. Leave for 6 weeks. After this time, remove some of the stones and crack them. Remove the kernels and skin them. Put kernels and broken shells back into the jar. Leave for 2–3 weeks. Strain through a filter paper. Dissolve the sugar in the water, bring to the boil and boil for 10 minutes. Let the syrup cool, then add it to the liqueur. Bottle and stopper tightly.

Orange Brandy

about ½ lb. finely peeled sweet-orange rind (without any pith)
½ lb. granulated sugar
1 teaspoon powdered coriander

Fill a jar with the orange peel. Add the sugar and coriander, and cover with brandy. Cover tightly. Leave to mature for 2 months. Shake the jar from time to time. Strain and filter. Bottle and cork down tightly. This can be added to cups and punches; it also makes a wonderful baste for chickens and ducks.

Peaches in Brandy

small just-ripe peaches
brandy

sugar syrup (allow 14 oz. sugar for each 1 lb. fruit and 1 pint water)

Wash the peaches, rub off the bloom with a clean rough cloth. Prick them with a silver or stainless steel fork. Make a syrup with the sugar and water. Boil until it thickens and is smooth. Put the peaches in the syrup, simmer for 6 minutes. Remove peaches and pack them into the jars, leaving plenty of room for the syrup and brandy. Pour in the syrup until the jars are about ¾ full. Leave to cool, then pour in the brandy up to the brim; shake to mix. Cover and seal. Leave for a few weeks, or longer, before trying.

The peaches can be chopped and served with ice cream with a little of the liqueur. They can be added to fruit salads and served with blancmanges, creams and jellies.

Raspberry Ratafia

raspberries
brandy

same quantity of sugar as fruit
1 gill water to 1 lb. sugar

Pick over and hull the raspberries. Put them in a jar, cover with brandy, leave them in a warm place for 1 month. Dissolve the sugar in the water, bring to the boil, then boil for 10 minutes. Strain the brandy and filter through paper. When syrup is cold, add it to the brandy. Bottle and stopper securely.

Rum Pot

The British have a version of Bachelors' Jam. They put rum in a pot, add fruit in season and sugar. There is also a German version called Rumtopf; one can buy specially designed crocks, with the name painted on, to make it in.

ADDITIONAL RECIPES

Ham and Apricot Rolls

Serves 4

8 *large slices of thinly carved boiled ham (spread with mustard)*

FOR THE FILLING

1 cup cooked rice
5–6 finely chopped sherried apricots (see page 203)
1 tablespoon sherry from the apricots
a few drops of Tabasco
freshly ground pepper
¼ teaspoon cinnamon
beaten egg

Mix the rice, apricots, Tabasco, pepper, cinnamon and sherry together, bind with the beaten egg. Put some of the filling on each slice of ham. Roll them up and fasten with toothpicks. Arrange the rolls in a shallow fireproof dish, cover with

Cambridge Apricot Tart

3 oz. butter
3 oz. castor sugar
yolks of 2 eggs

sherried apricots (see page 203)
approx. 6 oz. shortcrust pastry
  (see page 220)

Line a 7 in. flan tin with the pastry. Chop into quarters sufficient apricots to cover the base and arrange these in the pastry case. Melt the butter in a double saucepan, beat the sugar and egg yolks together and add to butter, together with one tablespoon of the apricot sherry. Bring the mixture almost to the boil, stirring well, then pour it immediately over the apricots. Bake in a moderately hot oven (375°F) until the top is golden and crinkly. This is best when eaten at once; if it is served later it should be gently warmed through.

Ginger Apricot Bavarois

FOR THE GINGER BISCUIT BASE

6 oz. ginger biscuits
3 oz. butter

1 tablespoon brown sugar

Put the biscuits in a bag and crush them with a rolling pin. Melt the butter, add the sugar, stir to mix, then add the crushed biscuits. Cover the base and sides of a serving dish approximately 8 in. diameter and 1¾–2 in. deep. Press the mixture down firmly. Put it in the refrigerator or a cool place until the crust hardens. Trim the edges.

MAKING AND USING LIQUEURS

TO MAKE THE BAVAROIS

- 4 eggs
- 4 oz. caster sugar
- 1 pint milk
- ½ oz. gelatine (*softened in a little cold water*)
- ½ pint lightly whipped cream
- 6–8 finely chopped sherried apricots (*see page* 203)
- 1 tablespoon sherry from the apricots

Separate the eggs. Beat sugar and yolks together until light. Boil the milk, add it gradually to the sugar and yolks. Pour it back into the saucepan, cook slowly and stir until the custard thickens. Heat the gelatine, with the sherry. Add it to the custard. Pour into a basin to cool, stirring constantly to prevent a skin forming. Beat egg whites stiffly. When the custard mixture begins to set, add the egg whites, cream and apricots. Stir lightly to mix.

TO ASSEMBLE AND DECORATE

walnut halves and quartered sherried apricots

Put the bavarois on top of the ginger biscuit base. Decorate with the walnuts and apricots. Serve chilled.

Miscellaneous

MINCEMEAT AND OTHER RECIPES

Mincemeat
Mincemeat without Suet
Christmas Mincemeat Ring

Mint Honey
Mushroom Ketchup

Mincemeat

Basically there is very little difference in the ingredients and making of mincemeat. You can add or subtract as you like. It is a variation of the Christmas theme of puddings and cakes, but instead of flour and eggs there is suet unless you make a vegetarian mincemeat which omits the suet. If you want it to keep well, add plenty of rum or brandy, or both.

1 lb. finely chopped beef suet
1 lb. Barbados sugar
1 lb. currants
1 lb. sultanas
1 lb. seedless raisins
½ lb. chopped candied peel
rind and juice of 2 large lemons
rind and juice of 2 oranges

2 oz. blanched, chopped almonds
1½ lb. peeled, cored and chopped cooking apples
1 oz. mixed spice
¼ oz. grated nutmeg
pinch of salt
1 gill rum or brandy

MISCELLANEOUS

Mix together all the ingredients, except the alcohol, put them in a covered bowl and leave for 3 days. Stir from time to time. Add the alcohol, mixing it thoroughly. Pack the mincemeat into jars, pushing the mixture down with a spoon to avoid air pockets. Put a waxed disc on, cover and store in a really dry place. Leave to mature for 2–3 weeks before using.

Mincemeat without Suet

1 *lb. unsalted butter*
1 *lb. Barbados sugar*
1 *lb. currants*
1 *lb. sultanas*
1 *lb. seedless raisins*
½ *lb. chopped candied peel*
rind and juice of 4 *lemons*
1½ *lb. peeled, cored and chopped cooking apples*
1 *oz. mixed spice*
¼ *oz. grated nutmeg*
pinch of salt
small wineglass of sherry
a jigger of brandy

Mix together all the ingedients, except the alcohol. Put them in a covered bowl and leave for 3 days. Stir from time to time. Add the alcohol, mixing in thoroughly. Pack the mincemeat into jars, pushing the mixture down with a spoon to avoid air pockets. Put a waxed disc on, cover and store in a really dry place. Leave to mature for 2–3 weeks before using.

Christmas Mincemeat Ring

8 *oz. plain flour*
2½ *teaspoons baking powder*
5 *oz. sugar*
5 *oz. butter*
1 *slightly beaten egg*
¾ *gill milk*
6 *oz. fruit mintemeat*
warm icing
glacé cherries and chopped nuts

MISCELLANEOUS

Sift flour, baking powder and sugar together. Rub in butter until mixture looks like breadcrumbs. Mix egg, milk and mincemeat together. Stir into the dry ingredients. Grease an 8 in. ring tin. Put in the mixture, bake for 40–45 minutes at 350°F. When cool ice with warm icing, decorate with cherries and nuts.

FOR THE WARM ICING

*4 oz. icing sugar**flavouring (see below)*
1 tablespoon warm water

If necessary, crush out any lumps in the sugar. Put it in a basin over hot water. Gradually add the warm water, stir until it is dissolved and the icing is smooth and warm all through. If it gets too hot it will not be glossy. Add flavouring. When the icing is the right texture it should coat the back of the spoon. If it is too thick, add more water; if too thin, add more icing sugar. Let it cool a little, then coat the Christmas ring.

FOR THE FLAVOURING

¼ teaspoon vanilla essence may be added or ½ teaspoon instant coffee

For lemon or orange flavour, substitute strained lemon or orange juice for the water.

Mint Honey

*plenty of freshly gathered mint**boiling water*
liquid honey

MISCELLANEOUS

Strip the mint leaves from the stems. Chop them finely, pour boiling water on them, leave for 4–5 minutes, drain well. Stuff the chopped mint into a jar about ¾ full of liquid honey. Put in as much mint as you can. Stir well to mix. Screw down and keep in a cool place. When you need mint sauce, take 2–3 spoonfuls of the mint and honey, and mix with wine vinegar or lemon juice to taste.

Mushroom Ketchup

If you can get field mushrooms do use them for this recipe; they have much more flavour then cultivated ones. If you have to use cultivated ones, try to get the large open ones now often seen in the shops.

It is the salt that extracts the essence of the mushrooms and preserves them. In Victorian times this ketchup was in most store cupboards and was used as a flavouring for sauces, soups and savoury dishes. Obviously it is very salty and must be used with discretion. It has a unique, exotic flavour, and can be used instead of soy sauce.

Wipe the mushrooms. Put a layer, including the stalks, in a bowl. Sprinkle coarse sea salt over them. Put another layer of mushrooms and salt on top. Continue in this way until you have used up the mushrooms. Leave for 4 hours. Break the mushrooms into pieces, (this is better done by hand), and put them in a cool place. Leave them for 3–4 days, stirring and pressing them with a wooden spoon to extract all the juice possible.

Measure the juice and mushrooms, and to each pint allow:

⅛ *oz. cayenne pepper*   ¼ *oz. ground ginger*
¼ *oz. allspice*   1 *blade of mace*

MISCELLANEOUS

Put all the ingredients into a heavy pan. Simmer gently for 30 minutes. Pour the mixture into a jug and leave it in a cool place overnight. The next day strain it into bottles. Empty vinegar or sauce bottles are ideal.

Appendix

USEFUL PASTRY RECIPES

Pâte Sucrée

This pastry is only suitable for sweet dishes. It is much richer than shortcrust pastry. When it is cooked let it cool in the pie plate, flan ring or patty pans. It is very friable and easily breaks.

8 oz. plain flour	3 oz. sugar
pinch of salt	2 egg yolks
4 oz. butter	

Sift flour and salt together. Cut the butter into small pieces, rub it lightly into the flour. Make a hole in the centre of the flour, add the sugar and egg yolks. Mix quickly but thoroughly. This paste should be quite firm. Leave for 1 hour at least in the refrigerator before using. Use as required.

Puff Pastry

8 oz. plain flour	1 gill ice-cold water (*it may not be necessary to use all the water and lemon juice*)
pinch of salt	
8 oz. unsalted butter	
½ teaspoon lemon juice	

Sift flour and salt together. Gradually add the water and lemon juice. It is better not to add this all in one go, as flours vary and some absorb more liquid than others. Mix together the flour and water with the finger tips or a wooden spatula. Knead until the paste no longer sticks to the fingers. This first dough should be firm rather than soft. Flour the board, roll the pastry out to a rectangle about ¼ in. thick. Cut the butter into small pieces, dot it all over the dough. Fold the dough in three. Press down the two open ends of the pastry with the rolling pin. This encloses the air. Roll out again (taking care the butter does not extrude) to a rectangle about ¼ in. thick, fold in three, press down open edges, give a half turn. Roll out again, fold in three. Leave in a cool place for 15 minutes. Repeat, fold, half turn three times. Leave overnight in the refrigerator.

Roll out and use as required. Puff pastry always needs a very hot oven (450–475°F) until it has risen, then the heat can be reduced. It depends on what you are making.

Shortcrust Pastry

8 oz. plain flour
pinch of salt

4 oz. butter (or 2 oz. butter and 2 oz. pure lard)
ice-cold water to mix

Sift the flour and salt together in a bowl. Rub in the butter (or butter and lard), lightly until it looks like coarse breadcrumbs. Add a little ice-cold water and mix to a stiff paste. Leave in the refrigerator or a cold place, overnight if possible; if not, chill as long as you can.

To use. Lightly flour a board or marble slab, and the rolling pin. Roll the pastry out quickly with short strokes. If any flour is left on the pastry, brush it off gently with a pastry brush.

When 8 oz. pastry is asked for in a recipe it means 8 oz. flour plus the other ingredients.

8 oz. pastry is needed for an 8–9 in. tart with pastry at the bottom and top.

8 oz. pastry makes about 16 small tarts.

4 oz. pastry will line a 7 in. pie plate or flan ring.

6 oz. pastry is needed to top a $1\frac{1}{2}$ pint pie dish.

Suet Crust

8 *oz. plain flour*
$\frac{1}{4}$ *teaspoon salt*
1 *teaspoon baking powder*

4 *oz. very finely chopped or shredded suet*
cold water to mix

Sift the flour, salt and baking powder together. Add the suet. Gradually add enough cold water to make a stiffish dough. Use as required.

How to line a Flan Ring

Lightly grease the baking tray and the ring. Roll out the pastry $\frac{1}{8}$ in. thick into a circle $1\frac{1}{2}$ in. larger than the ring. Lift the pastry up on the rolling pin (this avoids stretching the pastry) and line the ring. Press the pastry in lightly. Pass the rolling pin over the top to trim the edges. With a knife nick the pastry edge at regular intervals all round. Prick the base all over.

TO BAKE BLIND

Line the case with greased greaseproof paper, fill it with dry haricot beans. Bake at 375°F until the pastry is set (about

APPENDIX

9 minutes). Remove it from the oven, take out paper and beans. Brush the pastry bottom with lightly beaten egg white. This prevents the pastry from becoming soggy with the filling. Put it back in the oven to dry out and brown lightly.

Glossary

Albedo   Technical name for the white pith of citrus fruit. A source of pectin.

Baking Blind   Baking flan or tart cases without filling, to be used later.

Berries   Small fruit usually roundish, without stones, but with seeds enclosed in pulp.

Beurre Manié   Butter and flour worked together and added to hot liquids to thicken them.

Botulism   Poison caused by toxin-producing micro-organisms – Clostridium Botulinum. These organisms are sometimes found in soil. Non-acid vegetables require a very high temperature to kill the bacteria, which is not feasible in home bottling.

Brine   A salt solution.

Browning of Fruit   Cut fruit exposed to air oxydises and discolours.

Citrus Fruits   Members of the genus Citrus, characterised by tough peel, with separate sections divided by membranes. Includes lemon, orange, grapefruit, Kumquat, citron, lime, tangerine, etc.

Colloids   Particles larger than molecules, but not large enough to be visible. The large particles of proteins can be suspended in water to form viscous, sticky colloidal solutions.

Crystallisation   Crystals of a regular shape are formed when a

GLOSSARY

solution, particularly a saturated solution, evaporates without being disturbed; e.g., when a sugar or salt solution is reduced slowly without movement, solid crystals of a regular geometric shape are formed. Some Italian liqueurs have twigs in them, on which sugar crystallises out to form attractive patterns.

Drupes Fleshy fruits containing stones, such as peaches, plums, apricots and cherries.

Enzymes These are organic catalysts, i.e. chemicals which help reactions to take place, without being changed themselves in the process. The changes which they cause are in some cases necessary to life and development, but in other cases cause deterioration. Most of them – and there are hundreds of them – end in 'ASE' e.g. diastase is the enzyme which converts starch into sugar.

Flavedo The outer coloured rind of citrus fruits, also called the zest.

Fruit Jelly A fruit juice which has gelled with the help of pectin and sugar.

Gel A semi-solid substance containing a large quantity of water. It is colloidal.

Gelation The forming of a gel.

Gelling Point The temperature and concentration at which colloidal solutions solidify into a gel.

Glucose This is a sugar found in sweet fruits and honey, it is sometimes known as grape sugar. It is a good source of energy. Glucose is manufactured commercially from starch.

Grapes These are classified as a separate group of fruit.

Hermetic sealing The airtight closure of a vessel, so that it is completely isolated from the outside atmosphere. Therefore it cannot become contaminated.

Hydrometer This is an instrument for measuring the density of liquids. It can be used to measure the concentration of sugar in a solution. It consists of a slender glass-tube float with a scale on

GLOSSARY

it. It is weighted at the bottom to keep it upright. The depth to which it sinks in the fluid shows its density in comparison with water. Different types of hydrometers have different scales, so the instructions must be studied.

Invert Sugar This is a mixture of glucose and fructose. It is present in honey. When sugar is boiled with fruit, as in jam and jelly making, the acid present converts much of the sugar into invert sugar. This does not easily crystallise out.

Melons or Gourds A family of fruits with tough skin and flat seeds including melons, pumpkins and vegetable marrow.

Osmosis Liquids of different concentrations – densities – penetrate any porous barrier placed between them. The denser solution moves through the barrier and mixes with the other fluid until the concentrations are equal. This is important in the candying of fruit, etc., as it allows the sugar to penetrate through the skin.

Oxydisation or Oxydation A chemical action in which a substance combines with oxygen. Burning and rusting are examples. Fruits, such as cut apples and skinned bananas, oxydise when left in contact with the air; this turns them brown.

Pectins These are carbohydrates present in fruit, which enables fruit juices to form jellies. Their chemistry is very complex.

Pomes Fruits belonging to the Malaceae family, such as apples, quinces and pears.

Preservatives Commercial manufacturers use various forms of artificial preservatives to increase the keeping qualities of their products. In this book I do not recommend the use of any of these, as in the opinion of many they detract from the quality of a preserve.

Saturated Solution A given quantity of water, or other solvent, can only dissolve a finite quantity of a soluble substance, such as sugar. When it has dissolved as much as it can it becomes a

GLOSSARY

saturated solution. After this point, either solids will be left at the bottom or they will crystallise out.

Solution When a solid, such as sugar, becomes a fluid by being dissolved in water or other solvent, such as alcohol, it becomes a solution.

Sterilisation This renders a substance free from micro-organisms, by heat treatment or disinfectant.

Suspension This is when particles are suspended throughout a fluid without being dissolved in it.

Syneresis The technical term for a jelly 'weeping' – or the separation of a liquid from a gel.

Tisanes The French word for infusions made from dried flowers, leaves or plants. Some of these are supposed to have medicinal properties.

Vacuum This literally means an empty space. It is used to describe a vessel from which as much air as possible has been extracted.

Viscosity This is the word used to describe the resistance of a fluid to flow. The thicker a liquid, the greater its viscosity. It is measured by comparing the speed with which a fluid passes through a small hole in comparison with the flow of water.

Weeping of Jellies See syneresis.

Yeasts Living one-cell plants which cause fermentation. They are usefully employed in dough making, brewing and wine making. Some yeasts are present in the air and on plants, so that they must be excluded from preserves to prevent fermentation.

Index

Acidulated Water, 132
Albedo, 223
Alcohol, Preserving with, 199–211
Almond and Cherry Tart, 135
Andalusian Orange Marmalade, 98
Angelica Stalks, Candied, 117
Angel's Liqueur, 201
Apple
  and Banana Chutney, 158
  and Blackberry Jam, 37
  Butter, 52
  Conserve, Normandy, 35
  Jelly, Minted, 79
  and Lemon Curd Pie, 63
  Old Homestead Chutney, 157
  and Plum Jam, 45
Apricot
  Ginger Bavarois, 212
  and Ham Rolls, 211
  Jam, Dried, 36
  Jam, Fresh, 35
  Tart, Cambridge, 212

Bachelors' Jam (La Confiture de Vieux Garçons), 207
Baked Chutney Cheese Rolls, 179
Baked Meat Loaf, 185
Baking Blind, 223
Banana
  and Apple Chutney, 158
  Trifle, 58
Bar-le-Duc, 10, 36

Cream Cheese, 60
Gooseberry, 42
Basil (Sweet and Bush), 193
Batter, Coating, 60
  Pudding, boiled, 10, 187
Bay Leaves, 193
Bavarois, Ginger Apricot, 212
Béarnaise Sauce, 197
Beef Smoore with Peach Chutney, 10, 175
Beetroot, pickled, 164
Berliner Weisse, 146
Beignets, Jam, 62
Berries, 223
  Bottling, 130
Beurre Manié, 223
Bigarade Sauce, with Wild Duck, 10, 106
Bilberry Jelly, 75, 90
Blackberry and Apple Jam, 37
  Jelly, 75
  Jelly, G-M's Spicy Hot, 76
Blackcurrant
  Jam, 37
  Jelly, 76
  Liqueur, 204
  Rum, 204
  Tea, 69
Boeuf Gros Sel, 176
Boiled Batter Pudding with Raspberry Vinegar, 10, 187
Boiled Pork with Orange Sauce, 105
Bottled Fruit, Recipes Using, 135–6

227

INDEX

Bottling
  Apples, 132
  Berries, 130
  Drupes, 131
  Dry, Slow Oven Method, 133
  Fluids, 127
  Fruit, 129–36
  Pan, Fruit, 125
  Pears, 132
  Pomes, 132
  Pressure Cooker Method, 134
  Quick Water Pan Method, 129
  Quinces, 132
  Sub-Tropical and Tropical Fruit, 132
  Wet, Moderate Oven Method, 134
Botulism, 11, 225
Bouquet Garni, 176, 193
Brandy
  Cherry, 205
  Orange, 209
  Peaches in, 210
Bread and Butter Fritters, 59
  Pudding, 121
Briar or Dog Rose Jelly, 77
Brine, 223
Browning of Fruit, 223
Buns, Raspberry, 65
Butters, Fruit, 51

Cabbage, red pickled, 164
Cake, Rose Petal, 67
Cambridge Apricot Tart, 212
Candied
  Angelica Stalks, 117
  Grapefruit peel, 119
  Lemon Peel, 119
  Orange Peel, 119
  Frozen Fruit Custard, 122
Candying
  Fresh Fruit, 115
  Tinned Fruit, 113
  Syrup, using up, 117
Cardinal's Ghost (Kardinalgeist), 205
Carp, Connoisseur's, 179
Carrot and Almond Preserve, 38
Chamomile (Camomille), 194
Cheese
  and Chutney Baked Rolls, 179
  and Chutney Quiche, 177
  and Chutney Spread, 177
Cheeses, Fruit, 52
Cherry
  and Almond Tart, 135
  Brandy, 205
  Jam, Black, 38
  Jam, Imperial, 39
  Jam, Morello, 39
  White, and Orange Conserve, 44
  Pitter, 20, 127
  Sauce, 57
  Stalks (Queues de Cerises), 194
  Syrup, 140
Cherries in Spiced Vinegar, 164
Chervil, 193
Chestnut Jam, 40
Chestnuts, Marrons Glacés, 118
  Marronmarma Cream, 109
Chicken, Siamese Style, 10, 177
  Poulet à L'Estragon, 195
Chilli Sherry, 206
  Vinegar, 152
Chinese Sweet-Sour Mixed Fruit Chutney, 158
Chocolate Orange Matchsticks, 121
Christmas Mincemeat Ring, 215
Chutney Making (and Pickles)
  General Hints, 156
Chutney
  Apple, Old Homestead, 157
  Baked Meat Loaf, 185
  Banana and Apple, 158
  Cheese Rolls, Baked, 179

INDEX

Chutney—*cont.*
  Chinese Sweet-Sour Mixed Fruit, 158
  Fruit, Mixed, 159
  Gooseberry, 159
  Lemon, 161
  Lime, 160
  Mango, Green, 161
  Peach, Siamese, 162
  Pear and Lemon, 162
  Plum, 163
  Preserved Stem Ginger, 160
  Quiche, Cheese and, 10, 177
  Spread, Cheese and, 177
Citrus Fruits, 223
Clear Mixed Pickle, 168
Clove Carnation Ratafia, 206
Coconut Cream, to make, 178
Colloids, 223
Confiture de Vieux Garçons, 207
Connoisseur's Carp, 179
Corn, Indian Pickled, 165
Cotignac, 40
Crab Apple Jelly, 77
Crab and Pickle Canapés, 180
Cranberry Conserve, 41
Cream Cheese, Bar-le-Duc, 60
Creole Punch, 117, 122
Croûtes aux Cerises, 61
Crystallisation, 223
Crystallised Fruit, 112
Cumberland Sauce, 85
Curd Puffs, 61
Curds, Fruit, 52
Custard
  Egg, 59
  Ice cream, 66
  Raspberry Ice, 66

Damson Cheese, 53
Damsons, Pickled, 165
Dates, Pickled, 166
Deposit, 128
Dog Rose, or Briar Jelly, 77
Dried Herbs in the Kitchen, 193
Drupes, 224
  Bottling, 131
Duck, Roast Stuffed with Sweet-Sour Chutney, 181
  Wild with Bigarade Sauce, 10, 106

Eggs, in Baked Potatoes with Chutney, 182
Elderflowers (Sureau), 194
Elderberry Syrup, 141
Enzymes, 224
Equipment for
  Jam, Jelly and Marmalade Making, 19–21
  Bottling, 125–7
Extract
  First, 72
  Second, 73

Fennel, 193
Fermentation, 127
Fig, Dried and Rhubarb Jam, 49
Fish Cakes with Lemon Pickle, 182
Flake Test, 27
Flan Ring, How to Line, 221
Flavedo, 224
French Apple Tart, 91
Fritters
  Bread and Butter, 59
  Peach, 92
Four Fruit Marmalade, 100
Fruit, 21
  Bottling, 129–36
    Berries, 130
    Cold Water Pan Method, 133
    Dry, Slow Oven Method, 133
    Drupes, 131
    Pan, 125
    Pomes, 132
    Pressure Cooker Method, 134

INDEX

Fruit, Bottling—*cont.*
    Quick Water Pan Method, 129
    Sub-Tropical and Tropical, 132
    Wet, Moderate Oven Method, 134
  Browning of, 223
  Butters, 51
  Candied, Frozen Custard, 122
  Cheeses, 52
  Chutney, Mixed, 159
  Curds, 52
  Discoloration, 128
  Fresh, Candying, 115
  Jelly, 224
  Juices, 137–46
  Rising in Jar, 128
  Salad Tart (German Obstorte), 128
  Syrups, 137–46
Fruits
  Candied, 112
  Crystallised, 112
  Glacé, 112

Garlic Vinegar, 152
Gel, Gelation, Gelling Point, 19, 224
German Bowle, 205
German Obstorte (Fruit Salad Tart), 92
Gherkins, Sweet and Sour Pickled, 167
Ginger Apricot Bavarois, 212
Ginger and Marrow Jam, 43
Ginger Syrup, 142
Glacé Fruits, 112
Glaze, to make, 84, 94, 104
Glazed Sweet Potatoes, 104
Glucose, 22, 224
Gooseberry
  Bar-le-Duc, 42
  and Elderflower Jam, 43
  Chutney, 159
  Jam, 43
  Mint Jelly, 78
  Sauce, 56
Gourds, 225
Grapes, 224
Grapefruit Marmalade, 101
  Peel, Candied, 119
Gravy, for Hare Pudding, 87
  Orange, 106
Greengage Jam, 43
Green Mango Chutney, 161
Grenadine (Pomegranate Syrup), 144
Guards' Pudding, 62

Ham and Apricot Rolls, 211
  Glazed American Style, 84
  Minced with Cherry Sauce, 56
  Stuffed Marrow, 183
Hare Pudding, 86
Hedgerow Jelly, 78
Herbs
  Best Months for Drying, 192
  Dried, in the Kitchen, 193
  Recipes using, 195–8
Hermetic Sealing, 224
Hip and Haw Jelly, 79
Honey, Mint, 216

Ice Cream, Custard for, 66
Ice, Raspberry Custard, 66
Icing, Pink for Rose Petal Cake, 68
Indian Corn, Pickled, 165
Infusions (Tisanes), 194

Jam
  Apple Conserve, Normandy, 35
  Apricot, Fresh, 35
  Apricot, Dried, 36
  Bar-le-Duc, 10, 36
  Beignets, 82
  Blackberry and Apple, 37

INDEX

Jam—*cont.*
Blackcurrant, 37
Carrot and Almond Preserve, 38
Cherry, Black, 38
  Imperial, 39
  Morello, 39
Chestnut, 40
Cotignac, 40
Cranberry Conserve, 41
Dip Stick, To Make, 20
Funnel, 20
Gooseberry, 43
  Bar-le-Duc, 42
  and Elderflower, 42
Greengage, 43
Low Sugar, 50
Marrow and Ginger, 43
Mulberry, 44
Orange and White Cherry, 44
Passion Fruit and Peach, 45
Plum and Apple, 45
Pot Covers, 20, 29
Puffs, 61
Pumpkin Preserve, 46
Quince Jelly, 46
Raspberry, 47
  Seedless, 47
Red Rose Petal, 48
Rhubarb and Dried Fig, 49
  and Orange, 49
Strawberry, Common, 50
  Whole, 50
Turnovers, 63
Jars, 20
For Fruit Bottling, 126
Clip, 126
Screw Top, 126
Jelly
Bag, 20
Bilberry, 75
Blackberry, 75
  G-M's Spicy Hot, 76
Briar or Dog Rose, 76
Crab Apple, 77
Fruit, Definition of, 224
General Rules for Making, 72–4
Gooseberry, Mint, 78
Hedgerow, 78
Hip and Haw, 79
Lemon Marmalade, 102
Minted Apple, 79
Mulberry, 80
New England, 80
Orange Marmalade, 102
Quince, 10, 81
Redcurrant, 81
  Epicurean, 82
Rose Geranium, 83
Rowanberry, 83
Violet, 83
Weeping of, 226
Juice, Tomato, 145
Juices, Fruit, 137–9
Juniper Liqueur, 208

Ketchup, Mushroom, 217
  Tomato, 173
Kidney's, Vance's Stuffed, 90

Labelling, 30
La Confiture de Vieux Garçons (Bachelors' Jam), 207
Lamb
  Chops, Braised, 55
  Shoulder, Piquant Stuffed, 184
Lemon
  Chutney, 161
  Curd, 54, 63
  Curd and Apple Pie, 63
  Drink, 142, 143
  Jelly Marmalade, 102
  Pear Chutney, 162
  Peel, Candied, 119
  Pickle, 168
  Pickle, with Fish Cakes, 182
  Syrup, 142

INDEX

Lime
  Chutney, 160
  Flowers (Tilleul), 195
  Pickle, 167
  West Indian Marmalade, 103
Liqueurs
  Angel's, 203
  Blackcurrant, 204
  Juniper, 208
  Noyau, 209

Mango, Green Chutney, 161
Marjoram, 193
Marmalade
  Andalusian Orange, 98
  Dark Chunky, 99
  Family, 100
  Four Fruit, 100
  Grapefruit, 101
  Green Tomato, 101
  Lemon Jelly, 103
  Orange Jelly, 102
  Pressure Cooker, 103
  West Indian Lime, 103
  Recipe, Prototype, 98
  Sauce with Baked Pears, 108
  Tart, 108
Marronmarma Cream, 109
Marrons Glacés, 118
Marrow and Ginger Jam, 43
  Ham Stuffed, 183
Measures, Weights and, 12–14
Meat Balls with Pomegranate Soup, 196
  Loaf, Baked, 185
Melons, 225
Metric Equivalents, 12–14
Mincemeat, 214–15
  Christmas Ring, 215
  Without Suet, 215
Mint (menthe), 193, 195
  and Gooseberry Jelly, 78
  Honey, 216
  Sauce, 168
Minted Apple Jelly, 79
Mirlitons (Macaroon Tarts), 64
Mixed Pickle, Clear, 168
Morello Cherry Jam, 39
Mould, 127
Mulberry Jam, 44
  Jelly, 80
Mushroom Ketchup, 217
Mustard Sauce, Fruity, 120

Nasturtium Seeds, Pickled, 169
New England Jelly, 80
Normandy Apple Conserve, 35
  Pudding, 64
Noyau Liqueur, 209
  Raspberry, 67

Onions, Pickled, 171
Omelette, Poor Man's Baked, 65
Orange
  Brandy, 209
  Chocolate Matchsticks, 121
  Curd, 54
  Drink, 143
  Gravy, 106
  Jelly Marmalade, 102
  Marmalade, Andalusian, 98
  Peel, Candied, 119
  and Quince Preserve (Cotignac), 40
  and Rhubarb Jam, 49
  Sauce with Boiled Pork, 105
  Stuffed Pork Rolls, 105
  and Veal, 107
  and White Cherry Conserve, 44
Osmosis, 112, 225
Oven Temperatures, 13–14
Oxydisation or Oxydation, 225

Paraffin Wax, 20, 29
Parsley, 193
Partridges with Cherry Sauce, 57

INDEX

Passion Fruit and Peach Jam, 45
Pastry, 219
  Pâte Sucrée, 219
  Puff, 219
  Shortcrust, 220
  Suet Crust, 221
Peach Fritters, 92
  and Passion Fruit Jam, 45
  Siamese Chutney, 162
Peaches in Brandy, 210
Pear and Lemon Chutney, 162
Pears, Baked with Marmalade Sauce, 108
Pectin, 19, 23–6, 225
  Boosters, 24
  Content Test, 26
  Stock, 25
  Table, 24
Piccalilli, 169
Pickleburgers, 185
Pickles
  Beetroot, 164
  Cabbage, Red, 164
  and Chutney Making, General Hints, 156
  Damsons, 165
  Dates, 166
  Gherkins, Sweet and Sour, 167
  Indian Corn, 165
  Lemon, 168
  Lime, 167
  Mixed, Clear, 169
  Nasturtium Seeds, 169
  Onions, 171
  Pineapple, 172
  Rhubarb, 172
  Walnuts with Sweet Spiced Vinegar, 173
  Water Melon, 174
  with Welsh Rarebit, 186
Pie, Lemon Curd and Apple, 63
  Rabbit, 89
Pimientos Preserved in Vinegar, 171
  With Pork and Quince Jelly, 88
Piquant Stuffed Lamb Shoulder, 184
Plum and Apple Jam, 45
  Chutney, 163
Pomegranate Soup with Meat Balls, 196
  Syrup (Grenadine), 144
Pomes, 225
  Bottling, 132
Poor Man's Baked Omelette, 65
Pork
  Boiled with Orange Sauce, 105
  Chops with Quince Jelly, 87
  Rolls, Orange Stuffed, 105
  With Pimientos and Quince Jelly, 88
Potatoes, Baked with Eggs and Chutney, 152
Potting, 28–9, 156
Poulet à L'Estragon, 195
Preservatives, 225
Preserved Stem Ginger Chutney, 160
Preserving
  Alcohol, with, 199–213
  Drying, by, 189–98
  Sterilisation and Vacuum, by, 123–46
  Sugar, with, 17–146
  Vinegar and Spices, 147–88
  Pan, 20
Pressure Cooker Bottling Method, 134
Pressure Cooker Marmalade, 103
Pudding
  Boiled Batter with Raspberry Vinegar, 187
  Bread and Butter, 121
  Guards', 62
  Hare, 86
  Vermicelli, 109
Puff Pastry, 219

233

INDEX

Pumpkin Preserve, 46
Punch Creole, 122

Quince
  Cheese, 55
  Jelly, 10, 81
  Jelly Jam, 46
  Jelly with Pork Chops, 87
  Jelly with Pork and Pimientos, 88
  Orange Preserve (Cotignac), 60

Rabbit Pie, 89
Raspberry
  Buns, 65
  Custard Ice, 66
  Jam, 47
  Jam, Seedless, 47
  Noyau, 67
  Ratafia, 210
  Sauce, 62
  Syrup, 143
  Vinegar, 10, 154
Ratafia, Clove Carnation, 206
  Raspberry, 210
Red Cabbage, Pickled, 164
Redcurrant Jelly, 81
  Epicurean, 82
Rhubarb
  Dried Fig Jam, and, 49
  Orange Jam, and, 49
  Pickle, 172
Roast Stuffed Duck with Sweet-Sour Chutney, 181
Rolypoly, Rouen, 68
Rose
  Geranium Jelly, 82
  Hip Syrup, 144
  Petal Cake, 67
  Petal Conserve, Red, 48
  Vinegar, 154
Rosemary, 193, 195
Rouleau Rouennais, 68

Rowanberry Jelly, 83
Rum
  Blackcurrant, 204
  Pot, 211

Sage, 193
Saturated Solution, 225
Sauces
  Béarnaise, 197
  Bigarade, 106
  Cherry, 57
  Cumberland, 85
  Fruity Mustard, 120
  Gooseberry, 56
  Marmalade, 108
  Orange, 105
  Raspberry, 62
  Suprême, 196
  Walnut, 186
  White, 120
Saucer Test, 27
Savory, 193
Savoury Recipes Using
  Candied Fruits, 120
  Chutneys and Pickles, 175–86
  Jam, 55–8
  Jelly, 84–90
  Marmalade, 104–8
Setting, Tests For, 26
Shallot Vinegar, 153
Sherry
  Apricots in, 203
  Chilli, 206
Shortcrust Pastry, 220
Siamese Peach Chutney, 162
Solution, 226
  Saturated, 225
Spiced Vinegar, 153, 164, 174
Spices and Vinegar, Preserving with, 147–88
Spicy Water Melon Slices, 188
Sterilisation, 123–35, 226
Storage, 30

INDEX

Storing
  Candied Fruit, 115
  Chutneys and Pickles, 157
  Fruit, Bottled, 130
  Herbs, 192
Strawberry
  Jam, Common, 49
  Jam, Whole, 51
  Syrup, 143
  Tart, 93
Sub-Tropical and Tropical Fruit, 132
Suet Crust, 221
Sugar, 22
  Concentration, 19
  Invert, 225
  Syrup, 127
  Temperatures, 15
  Thermometer, 15, 27
Suspension, 226
Sweet Potatoes Glazed, 104
Sweet Recipes Using
  Bottled Fruit, 92, 135
  Candied Fruit, 121, 122
  Jam, 58–69
  Jelly, 91–4
  Marmalade, 108–9
  Vinegars and Pickles, 187–8
Sweet-Sour Mixed Fruit Chutney, 158
Sweet and Sour Pickled Gherkins, 167
Sweet Spiced Vinegar, 174
Syneresis, 226
Syrups
  Cherry, 140
  Elderberry, 141
  Ginger, 142
  Lemon, 142
  Orange, 143
  Pomegranate (Grenadine), 144
  Raspberry or Strawberry, 143
  Rose Hip, 144

Tarragon, 193
  Chicken with Suprême Sauce, 195
  Vinegar, 153
Tarts
  Cherry and Almond, 135
  French Apple, 91
  Marmalade, 108
  Strawberry, 93
Tea, Blackcurrant, 69
Temperatures
  Oven, 13–14
  Sugar, 15, 21, 27
Tests
  Flake, 26–8
  Fruit for Pectin Content, 26
  Saucer, 27
  for Setting Point, 26
  Sugar Thermometer, 27
  Volume, 27
Thyme, 193
Tilleul (Lime Flowers), 195
Tisanes (Infusions), 194, 226
Tomato
  Juice, 145
  Ketchup, 173
  Marmalade, Green, 101
Trifle, Banana, 58
Turnovers, Jam, 63

Vacuum, 226
  Seal, Broken, 128
Vance's Stuffed Kidneys, 90
Veal and Orange, 107
Vegetables, Bottled, 11
Vermicelli Pudding, 109
Vervain (Verveine), 195
Vinegar
  Chilli, 152
  Fruit, 154
  Garlic, 152
  Making, 151
  Raspberry, 154

INDEX

Vinegar—*cont.*
  Rose, 154
  Spiced, 153, 164
  Spiced, Sweet, 174
  and Spices, Preserving with, 147–88
  Violet, 154
Vinegar Mother, 151
Violet Jelly, 83
Viscosity, 226
Volume Test, 20, 27

Walnut Sauce, 186
Walnuts, Pickled with Sweet Spiced Vinegar, 173

Water, 23
  Acidulated, 132
Water Melon Pickle, 174
  Slices, Spicy, 188
Weeping of Jellies (Syneresis), 226
Weights and Measures, 12–14
Welsh Rarebit with Pickles, 186
West Indian Lime Marmalade, 103
White Sauce, 120
Wild Duck with Bigarade Sauce, 106
Witches' Froth, 69

Yeasts, 226
Yield, 28

2 TINS PEACHES = 1lb 2oz Fruit
MAKES 5 lb. JAM INC 1 Kg Sugar

---

6 TINS PEACHES (410g)
2 Kg. SUGAR, 3 TBSP. LEMON JUICE
1 KNOB OF BUTTER
1 jar CERTO.
MAKES APPROX. 8 lb JAM.

---

8 TINS
2 KG. SUGAR.   MAKES APPROX 9 lb
